Contents

Part 5: Resourcing Homework and Study Support

Part 6: Sharing Information about Homework

Preface

Most schools try to get pupils to do homework, and to get teachers to set homework. Schools today use homework in many different ways, and in the 1990s it has become a political issue, too, with local and national policies being developed, and high-profile charitable contributions to the field. It is used to complement and supplement the classroom experience, to promote strategies of independent learning, to finish off class work, to punish children, to get homes/families involved in education, to incorporate hobbies and leisure pursuits into school work, to research for GCSE coursework, and, no doubt, to fulfil many other functions. However, the effort schools put in to homework is much less than that put into classwork. Much less time is spent justifying, planning for, and supporting homework than is spent on classwork. This book should help justify homework, though it isn't a manifesto, and will look at many ways of planning and supporting homework. Whether a school or a teacher is setting homework just because they have to, or for positive educational reasons, the homework set can be made more interesting, more appropriate, easier to complete or mark, more challenging, better preparation for class work, and so on. This book is centred on such improvements.

Looking at books for teachers and for parents, I'm often surprised how many assume that anyone wanting to develop their skills will want to increase the time they spend on them. I have tried to write a book that will help people *save* time, or help them make better use of their time, and not feel guilty about how little time they spend.

It can be difficult helping teachers, and even harder helping parents, because they have their own ways of teaching and bringing up children. I've tried to allow for these differences, and have written this book in the way that my favourite recipe books are written: enough practical ideas that can be followed mechanically, when feeling lazy; enough stimulating ideas that can provide inspiration, when feeling creative. Good luck with my ideas, and with your own.

My ideas are based on years of teaching various subjects in schools and universities, setting homework just about every day. Sadly, much homework (even some of my own, as my students will tell you) is of little use. I believe, though, that homework can be an exciting and effective way of learning. What would make me really happy, therefore, would be a change in people's attitudes to homework. The most important attitude of all is that learning, at home or in school, should be worthwhile and interesting, and not a stressful chore.

Different parts of this book are aimed at teachers, managers, and parents. The book explains why homework is important, how teachers can set interesting and effective and well-differentiated homework, how schools can best support homework, how managers can best develop whole-school homework policies, and how parents can support the educational progress of their children. Managers, advisors, librarians, and Primary school teachers might read every chapter; subject specialist teachers might read 26 of the chapters; parents might read nine chapters and look at the rest. But pupils do not have a section to themselves, apart from a brief guide in Chapter 32. There are two reasons for this. Firstly, pupil perspectives will I hope affect every section of the book, rather than be pushed into a corner. Secondly, I shudder to think of some poor pupil being forced to read a chunk of this book as an extra homework. Imaginative pupils may want to read to their parents the section saying how hard coursework is, and may want to tell teachers about the advantages of setting interesting homework. But really, I'd like us, the so-called responsible ones, to sort out what we do about homework, and let the little darlings have some fun.

Julian Stern
London
September 1996

Acknowledgements

The Open University's electronic conferencing system allowed me to exchange ideas with teachers, tutors and, especially, student teachers all around the country: their contributions and comments were invaluable. London University's Institute of Education provided me with opportunities over several years to work on homework with students and practising teachers. Camden LEA and the Prince's Trust, jointly, let me work in and manage a Homework Centre, and swap ideas with similar centres elsewhere in London, Liverpool, Glasgow, Bradford and Belfast. Teachers and pupils in Stockholm, especially Östra Reals Gymnasium, gave me many insights into the similarities and differences between UK and Swedish approaches to homework. Phil Salmon and Jean Jones have continued setting me homework, long after I thought I'd finished with it, and always make it worthwhile.

Teachers can learn from any school, especially their own, and from any teacher, parent, or pupil, and I wouldn't want to encourage a 'Cook's Tour' view of good practice in setting and supporting homework. The work of John MacBeath, which has done more than anything else to make this book possible, includes detailed studies of many good schools, for those wanting a tour.

Marie Stern and Pam Rauchwerger both improved the book in many ways. I'd like to dedicate this book to them and to all those other people who were too busy to bother about homework, but who did bother. Amongst those who contributed individual homework tasks or other useful ideas are Loredana Akhtar, Saira Barakzai, Linda Bjerninge, Rhian Evans, Linda French, Hazel Hanus-Haim, Anton Harvey, Gail Holden, Andy Hudson, Ursula Jeakins, Marie Nordin, Lisa Segerstedt, Robert Smith, Karl Stern, Naomi Strachan, Caroline Tamm, Donna Vaughan, Brian Weller, Anna Wengelin. All the jokes and all the mistakes are mine.

Part 1
What is Homework and What is it For?

CHAPTER 1

An introduction to the history, purpose and current use of homework in schools

Some pupils have asked me why they have to do homework. They have the wrong question. The peculiar thing is schoolwork, not homework. To learn, we don't always need teachers — certainly not in the sense we now think of teachers. Every language, I'm told, has a word for 'learning'. Not every language has a word for 'teaching'. As a professional teacher, I find that disturbing. All this time, I've thought that my pupils, my students, needed me. They couldn't do without me, and without me would sink into a poor, nasty, brutish and short, if not solitary, existence. I was the responsible one, the necessary bringer of order and good sense. Heads often think the same way about their teachers, as do parents about their children. The vanity of teachers, managers, and parents, is perpetuated by their pupils, staff, and children. However, just as our physical vanity can be disturbed by an accidental view of ourselves in the mirror, so our professional vanity can be disturbed by an accidental view of pupils, staff, children, acting responsibly on their own. I've walked past a room of quietly studious pupils, and thought how I wished they were one of my classes, only to find that they were indeed one of my classes; envying the skills of their teacher, I look again to see who it is, only to find that there isn't a teacher there. The worst thing is that if I walk in to see the class, there will be a cheer, or a groan, an increase in the noise and a decrease in the work, as the pupils revert to their roles as irresponsible, difficult, people.

Through most of history, people learnt from their families, amateurs as teachers, and from their peers and their colleagues. A small number of religious and political leaders might influence thousands or millions of followers or opponents, but the prime teachers of politics and religion were local people with other things to do. Learning kept going with or without professionals. As mass media, multi-media now, have been developed, books, television and computers have become sources of learning, sources of information, skills, languages, attitudes, culture, beliefs, propaganda, and much else. Learning, again, but not quite teaching as we teachers think of it. How long have professional teachers been around? The age of universal schooling, provided by professional teachers, has lasted no more than a century in this country, less elsewhere. The age when everyone expects a decade or more of education, alongside a lifetime of learning, is a bit of an historical oddity. It may even be about to end, although I think, myself, that there's too much else at stake to let half a million teachers free on the streets of Britain.

Homework, or at least work outside the influence of a professional teacher, is therefore ancient and venerable. For thousands of years, homework has been what everyone did: school work has been left to a tiny proportion of the population, from academicians in the Ancient world through the Medieval schools and universities. The very word 'homework' used to mean manufacturing work done at home rather than in a factory or workshop, and it meant this for a couple of hundred years before it was used to refer to school-set exercises. Even earlier, before factories spread, just about all work was done at home, and nothing distinguished 'manufacturing' from 'domestic chores'. The same goes for learning, before mass schooling was developed. It was done amongst all the other everyday tasks. Learning is an everyday activity, and this needs to be stressed to everyone, young and old, learner and teacher.

If there's one theme of this book, it is to try to remind schools of the spirit of learning outside school, the pleasure and excitement of learning outside the classroom. A recent survey suggested that 50% of children enjoyed school, but only 2% enjoyed homework. Some people feel that homework is a test of power of schools over pupils, an unpleasant chore, rightly hated. I'd like to counter that feeling. Homework can be what learning is at its best: grabbing hold of the world and making it make sense for you. How many adults still have, hidden away, some piece of work done years ago at school — a project on the Incas, or a story for the school magazine. Of all the 'kept' pieces of work, how many were done mostly or entirely at home? I'd like to bet 90% of them. Of all the studying done by teachers, at colleges and universities, most remembered is the dissertation done in the library and in college rooms, not the lectures and tutorials. Are you more fluent in the language you learnt in the classroom, or the language you learnt at home, aged nothing, or on holiday? There's a good basis for promoting homework, then, as the most exciting, memorable, side of education.

It would be foolish, of course, to ignore the negative side of homework. It can be a meaningless task set by a bored teacher who doesn't really care whether or not the homework is completed. It can be left to the last minute, and completed thoughtlessly, and involve little learning. It can hang over teachers, as much as pupils, as a routine bureaucratic task, a relief if it is not required. For that image of homework, this book may be an antidote. On the other hand, perhaps some poor teacher will be given this book and told to read it for homework. Apologies in advance.

When it comes to homework, I often sound like an abolitionist. Much homework is pointless, inefficient or a stressful burden on pupils. We would be surprised if a pupil or teacher brought their ironing in to school, on the grounds that they didn't have enough time to do it at home. Ironing and other housework is probably best done in the house. Similarly, school work should in general be done in school, not at home, and where homework is set, it should involve work that could not easily be done in school. So, for example, a good homework might be one that involved interviewing older relatives about their past experiences, or one that involved recording the pupil's eating habits for a week. The sort of homework that is just an extra bit of school work (but one not requiring the presence of a teacher) could often better be done in school, for example in an after-school club or open-access learning centre. It would be much more efficient for communities to fund such after-school facilities than the heating, lighting, or child-care costs of having pupils go straight home, worrying about homework. I'm not really an abolitionist. But schools have to think carefully about why, exactly, they set homework, and if they don't tackle this deep issue, they are unlikely to gain agreement from teachers, pupils and families about what homework to set.

CHAPTER 2

Homework related to wider issues of supporting study, independent learning, distance learning and flexible learning

For schools to get involved in improving the quality of learning, they may wish to start by making a list.

Pupils can learn better if

- they enjoy the work;
- they know what they are doing;
- their teacher knows what they are doing;
- the work is challenging;
- the work is not impossible;
- they have the facilities to complete the task;
- they have someone to ask if they get stuck;
- they have chosen some aspect of the task or course;
- they are happy, and not being bullied or harassed;
- the work is, or is seen as, relevant or useful;
- they will get something out of the work;
- they understand the reasons for doing the work;
- praise is given for work when done;
- their peers are all doing or trying to do the work, too.

Any group of teachers or pupils could probably add to the list, and could make a whole list of their own. What is interesting about such lists is that they show how complex learning is.

Learning is complex, so supporting learning, in school or at home, is also inevitably complex. Developing knowledge is part of it, for example, but it has become an educational cliché that, whatever we teach them today, our children will need new skills or information tomorrow. Facts may be fun, and should not be underestimated, but learning also includes learning how to learn, and how to deal with conflicting perspectives and opinions, and how to develop new skills, and how to apply old skills to new situations, and how to motivate yourself and other people. For a few years after 1988, schools were understandably obsessed with the covering of 'facts' in the National Curriculum. However, the quality of learning as a whole has, thank goodness, recently been put back at the centre of school plans. Schools have at last got back to thinking about how pupils learn — the stuff of teacher training courses, forgotten on qualification. I was lucky, and after teaching for years got involved in spare-time teacher training, and realised that some 'learning theory' was really quite useful. Schools are now, often, at that same stage.

Supporting learning, then, means more than providing extra information. It includes improving the motivation of pupils, reducing blocks to learning put up by bullying or racism, getting pupils to help each other, setting hard but achievable work, and much else. Homework, just like classwork, needs to be looked at in this broad way. Many teachers are careful to set carefully differentiated work in class, but set a homework task that is meaningless to, or impossible for, a significant number of pupils. They think about how to distribute resources around the classroom, but forget about the inequality of resources in pupils' homes. A chain is only as strong as its weakest link; perhaps the educational experience of pupils is only as good as its worst element: homework, as often as not. Improving the quality of learning has to include an imaginative review of homework. In some schools, this started with 'independent learning' initiatives.

Learning is about gaining independence, so the promotion in recent years of 'independent learning' should have come as little surprise. The reasons for looking at learning in this way came out of changes in the education of older pupils and students. Vocational and pre-vocational courses, not to mention pressures on staff time, encouraged learning that went beyond the classroom, that involved choices made by students about their own progress. So-called 'fofo' work, in which students go off and find out, was the sort of work that teachers and lecturers were setting up: pupils would leave the classroom to complete visits, surveys, interviews, and other fieldwork, using the classroom as a base in which to write up results and seek guidance from other students and staff. As students became adept at fofo work, the distinction between classwork and homework started to disappear. Students who could do fofo work could do homework just as easily as classwork, without the need for any further specific guidance.

The extreme version of such independent learning is distance learning. It is the Open University that is most associated with distance learning. Students may see their tutor once a month, perhaps once a term, yet the courses get completed and the students often feel very well supported. Since 1994 it has been possible to qualify as a teacher through the OU, with no more than nine 'classroom sessions' (tutorials and day schools) for the whole 18-month course. This is true independent learning, made possible by the support of mentors in schools, yet with such little formal tutoring. The proportion of time spent with tutors to time spent studying is very low: around 24 hours of tutor time to 440 hours of study, or 1:18. For OU courses, homework is clearly more than an 'add on': it is the centre-piece of the whole institution.

As well as OU courses, there are other effective models of distance learning. There is a whole world of correspondence courses, and there is the rather unfashionable world of instrumental tuition. I still remember my piano lessons, and can still more or less play the piano, but the lessons were only for an hour a week, much less time than I spent on French or Physics, both of which have left far less of an impression on me. Typically, instrumental tuition involves about one hour a week of 'lessons' and an hour a day of practising: a ratio of 1:7. Again, this implies that homework is more important than it seems to many school teachers. What makes the OU ratio of 1:18, or the instrumental ratio of 1:7 possible, when History teachers like myself find it difficult to get pupils to do half an hour of homework a week to support between one and two hours of lessons? The average school classwork to homework ratio is around 3:1. English teachers, for example, set an average of one hour 10 minutes of homework a week to year 9 pupils (according to Rutter *et al*, 1979), and they would be lucky if the pupils did that much. So why is it so difficult?

Take a long walk, or run, or cycle. Just as you arrive home, to a comfortable sofa and a good evening on the television, tell yourself to go for another long walk. Hard, isn't it? Instead, have a warm-up session before doing anything else, get your muscles toned up, your joints supple. Then go for a long walk. Isn't that easier? Schools usually treat classwork like a long walk, with homework as the extra walk. The OU, correspondence courses, and instrumental tutors, treat classwork like the warm-up, and homework like the walk. Independent learning is made possible by the second way of approaching learning. When independent learning is complemented by student choice or power, so that the teacher has a more modest role, then it becomes flexible learning. And with flexible learning, homework becomes something that will be chosen by students. Many school pupils would volunteer to do homework on a topic that they had chosen and had some control over. Once someone has joined a sports team, paid for membership to a fitness club, or entered for a marathon, watch them exercise. We can move from homework as drudgery to exciting homework, by moving from classwork as intellectual force-feeding to that of independent, flexible, learning.

CHAPTER 3

Homework and equal opportunities: the forgotten year

'Over the five years of secondary education, appropriate homework can add the equivalent of at least one additional year of full-time education' (Hargreaves, 1984). If we believe in equal opportunities, in giving all pupils a good education, what can we do to make sure that all pupils get the education they deserve, and avoid the loss of the 'homework year' suffered by so many pupils? Teachers would be appalled if a large group of pupils missed a day a week of school, or if they missed all the lessons in two of their subjects, for several years. Yet teachers are rarely surprised if they hear that a pupil has done no homework for years, or a class has been set no homework for years. I've been told by teachers that there's no point setting certain pupils homework, because they simply wouldn't do it, or couldn't do it. It would be more trouble than it was worth, it would cause too much trouble, even to ask. Now I'm not unsympathetic to such views, and I've often enough found hassling pupils for homework the least pleasant part of my relationship with a class. What really concerns me is that, whilst homework is ignored for some pupils or classes, other pupils or classes are expected to do large amounts of homework. If a large number of pupils can do no homework, we should just abolish it. That would provide equal, if fewer, opportunities for all.

Abolishing homework is a good, at least an interesting, idea. If we abolished homework, pupils might have more equal opportunities, as all their work would be done in school, under similar conditions, with less advantages given to those pupils with desks and encyclopaedias at home. A school that sets no homework might have more tightly organised lessons, as teachers could no longer say 'finish this at home', and pupils might have less stress, not worrying all evening about homework they should be doing. However, such a school would also be under pressure to extend its day, as there is little chance that a school with no homework could get the same amount of work done as a school with homework. Rather than extending the school day by adding lessons, the school might instead have extra sessions of relatively independent study, during which pupils would do what would otherwise have been set as homework. Of course, this has already been done: many boarding schools have 'prep' instead of homework, with an hour or two of supervised private study at the end of lessons. If we abolished homework, then, we would reinvent it — as suggested in a newspaper article, 'Down with homework — bring back prep!' (TES, November 1987).

Suppose that every school decided to abolish homework, as has happened in several countries: would that provide more equal opportunities, and a less stressful life for pupils? Perhaps, but I'm quite convinced that abolishing homework would be an illusion. Homes and families would help their children with their work, whether or not formal homework was set. Some homes and families would be able to help more than others, and issues of equal opportunities would again arise. Abolishing homework would I think be as inequitable as abolishing compulsory education: education itself would not be abolished, just the educational opportunities of a large portion of the population. Equal opportunities requires some homework, then, simply to formalise and make more equitable the help that may be given to pupils outside school.

Equal opportunities are often dealt with in parts, covering systematic inequalities in society. With respect to gender and homework, girls and boys may be encouraged to have different expectations in different subjects, and may have access to different forms of peer support and different career opportunities. There is no simple pattern. Girls may get less support with homework (I have seen some evidence of this), and may have more household tasks expected of them. Yet the introduction of GCSEs with assessed coursework (most often done as homework) has been offered as an explanation for girls overtaking boys in terms of achievements at 16. In monitoring homework teachers should see if certain types of task are completed more successfully by boys or girls, and try to set a variety of tasks, and offer a variety of support, so that all pupils can thrive.

When it comes to homework and ethnicity, stereotypes still run free. Teachers seem to find it easy to say of an ethnic group that families are unsupportive, or are over-ambitious, or treat girls as inferior. This can be recognised as absurd when we try to describe the home circumstances of the majority ethnic group, in many statistics named as white English Scottish Welsh and Irish or 'ESWI'. Are ESWI parents supportive or not, ambitious for their children or not? Are ESWI children keen on homework or not? Of course, some are and some are not. The same goes for every ethnic group. Equal opportunities in this context means setting homework that can be seen as relevant to to the lives and needs of all the pupils, and setting tasks that don't exacerbate the racism that pupils may come across. For example, heroes for some may be villains for others. Researching biographies is a popular homework task, but insensitive references to ambiguous figures can cause problems: teachers may be unaware of how Cromwell is regarded by many Irish people, or how deep feelings may be aroused by celebrating the execution of Guy Fawkes, or commiserating on the fatwa on Salmon Rushdie. It is not that contradictory opinions should be balanced in such a way that no one can have heroes, but rather that tasks should allow for a variety of opinions on who the 'real' heroes are. Describing alternative views, for homework, is good preparation for a future class debate, anyway. Why not ask how Christians, Jews, Muslims and atheists might regard the birth of Jesus?

Class is the third of the big equal opportunities sub-topics. There are still wider gaps between the achievements of pupils from different social classes than there are between those of any other groups. Class affects facilities available to pupils, and a simple way to address these differences is to provide good facilities for all pupils, the philosophy behind many Homework Centres, described in Chapter 28. Beyond this, homework that only addresses a narrow range of skills may favour one class over another. Extended writing tasks must be set for all pupils, but if nothing else is set, the teacher may be disadvantaging some pupils. I've been pleasantly surprised when I've set aural homework tasks, that different pupils achieve at different levels, to those achieved in written homework. Providing more equal opportunities, in this way, simply means providing more opportunities.

On all such issues, there are specialist accounts of how to tackle inequalities and discrimination on the grounds of sex, ethnicity and class. What I'd emphasise here is that inequalities may have even more influence on homework than classwork, and that there appear to be even bigger gaps between the time spent on homework by different pupils than there are between attendance rates in school. For many pupils in Secondary school, homework is a forgotten year: forgotten by teachers as well as pupils. I will return to issues of equal opportunities in later chapters, including Chapters 27–29 on how facilities outside the classroom might be organised and enhanced. Special needs are also related to access and opportunities, and they are the topic of the next chapter.

CHAPTER 4

Homework and special needs

Perhaps the most important issue in organising homework is to take account of the different skills of different pupils. Differentiation, or taking account of these differences, is vital in homework, and this book should be useful for those concerned with differentiation, special needs, and the education of pupils not yet fluent in English. Gone are the days of pupils with Statements of Special Needs getting no homework, on the grounds that they were incapable of it. (The examples of homework policies and guides in Chapters 31 to 33 were all written originally for a Special School.) Yet many still do little or no homework. Thinking about homework can help us think about special needs, and thinking about homework for pupils with special needs can help us think about homework for all pupils.

Special Educational Needs (SEN) includes pupils who are 'behind' (in some sense) their peers with their learning, unless the lag is a result of having English as a second or subsequent language. Some schools use the shorter phrase 'Special Needs'. This is sometimes a way of grouping together SEN and Bilingual support, and sometimes a way of including 'gifted' children. 'Gifted' children (or 'pupils of marked ability') are those who are significantly *ahead of* (in some sense) their peers. Very able pupils may have special needs — they may need an adapted curriculum to bring out their best efforts. In this chapter, I will say 'special needs' when referring to all pupils who fit any of these categories, and 'SEN' when referring to those (roughly 20% of all pupils) in the narrower category defined over the years by the Warnock Report, the 1981 Education Act, and the 1994 Code of Practice. A 'statemented' pupil belongs to a sub-group of pupils with SEN (roughly 2% of all pupils), who require a formal statement of their needs, negotiated and produced by a panel of teachers, educational psychologists, parents/carers, the local authority, health and often social services, and, in most cases, the pupil.

Here are three ways in which homework can help us think about special needs, and special needs can help us think about homework.

- The approach a pupil has to homework may help in the diagnosis of special needs. Pupils may demonstrate skills in their homework that are rarely shown in classwork: they may be bullied or harassed in class, and good homework might be a sign of a block to learning in class. (It may also be a sign of cheating, or even of bullying other pupils into doing the homework for them.) Pupils may do very little homework, and on being asked why, may admit that they understand little of the lessons and perhaps copy much of the classwork. Lack of homework might indicate difficult home circumstances. A superb piece of independent research might indicate considerable untapped learning potential. The quality of a pupil's homework might be a sign of the pupil's stress level or self-esteem. As homework is a common 'stressor', when a pupil is under stress from other circumstances, homework may well 'give'. (For teachers, marking/report writing often 'give' when the teacher is under most stress.) Special needs are often unrecognised, and if a teacher thinks a pupil may have particular special needs, individual homework tasks may be set to help with the diagnosis. For example, a pupil who is hard of hearing could be set a task of transcribing a short conversation (from a tape or video): if consonants (especially the letter 's', and the endings of words) are systematically missed out, then this is further evidence of poor hearing. (The classroom, full of noise and distractions, is not always a good place to test hearing!) There are other more or less formal diagnostic tests and exercises that might be set as homework. As parents or carers are involved in the statementing process, it makes sense to make use of homework as a way of improving communication between school, pupil, and home, covering the learning development of the pupil.
- Pupils can be set homework that helps them to develop or practise skills that are difficult to focus on in a classroom. Classrooms are ideal for common tasks (listening to a reading, doing an experiment, doing a close observation study of a still life), and for pupils developing cooperative group-work skills with their peers (brainstorming, debating, acting, producing a display). Homework, on the other hand, is ideal for specialised pupil-centred tasks (practising 'gh' spellings, doing exercises to help fine-motor skills, adding to a list of translations between English and the home language), for individuals exploring issues or skills in depth (projects and coursework), and for pupils developing cooperative work skills with people of different generations (interviewing grandparents about past times, 'consumer testing' a toy for a four year old). A full review of a pupil's special needs should include evidence from the whole range of activities, including those done at home.
- Catering for special needs means catering for variety. If the teacher

realises that a homework task is right for the 'middle' of the class, but will be too difficult or easy for several pupils, then there are two strategies. Either different homework can be set for pupils with different skills — fiddly, perhaps, but easier to manage as homework than as classwork. Or the original homework can be scrapped in favour of one that stretches and interests all the pupils. There are lots of examples of these later in this book. What I would recommend for a busy school is finding or creating a small number of brilliant homework tasks, within each subject, that stretch and interest all pupils, so that at least once or twice a term, in every subject, the pupils will get a good experience out of homework. (Better still if every homework is brilliant, but things don't always work that way.) Special needs are rarely 'general' — few pupils have difficulties with all aspects of learning, or have marked abilities in all areas — so having a policy of varying homework, week by week, can allow more needs to be catered for. A 'learning' homework might allow some to show their best qualities, an aural/oral homework might inspire others; a research task could support some, a tightly-structured task could support others.

- Resources are important to giving a good education to pupils with special needs. A pupil who needs to use a word processor in class, will in general also need it for homework. A pupil who needs careful supervision and a clear set of rules and procedures to help them cope with working in class may also need careful supervision when it comes to homework. Those pupils who get through textbooks and libraries at a rate of knots may need access to vast amounts of information to stretch them when it comes to homework. Resources may be provided for the home – portable computers, access to the Internet, and so on. Or schools may make those same resources available in school but outside lesson times — as in a Homework Centre. I've seen Statements include attendance at a Homework Centre: the people who wrote the Statement believing it could go a long way to meeting the pupils's SEN.

After thinking about special needs, it should be obvious that strategies (of differentiation, specialisation, variety and so on) that help with special needs will also help every pupil. J D Clare writes well about this, in a book *The Twentieth Century: Options in History Programme of Study* about History teaching, but applicable to many subjects and to most homework. He says that "differentiation by task is divisive, and not very successful. It is more effective to set open-ended tasks which can be tackled at different levels by pupils of different abilities, or series of tasks, where pupils of greater ability can progress further." It is important to point out that good, exciting, relevant, well-resourced, differentiated, homework tasks will almost inevitably be supportive for pupils with and without SEN, for monolingual and bilingual pupils, and for more or less gifted children. There are not *four* ways to teach well (one way for each 'special' category, and one way for 'the rest'), but *one* way.

Part 2
A Teachers' Guide to Homework

CHAPTER 5

Introduction: Setting, monitoring and assessing homework

Teachers take planning lessons for granted, yet when it comes to homework, most are happy with last-minute, badly thought-out, tasks of no great interest to anyone. There are issues of planning, timing, monitoring and chasing up homework, all of which worry most teachers. For example, if I ask teachers what problems their pupils have with homework, they usually say 'not understanding it'. If I ask teachers when would be the worst possible time to set homework, bearing in mind the fact that many pupils will not understand the task, they will say 'at the end of the lesson'. Not surprising. Then I read (MacBeath and Turner, 1990) about a study that found nearly all (94%) of homework was given at the end of the lesson, half of the time after the bell had rung, and often enough (in 9% of cases) during the ringing of the bell. One in 11 homework tasks really is set during the ringing of the bell, and most of the rest just either side of it. Despite teachers knowing the problems this may cause, they do indeed tend to set homework at the worst possible time.

Homework should be planned at the same time as you plan classwork. Whatever level of planning blight exists for lesson plans, it is worse for homework. Yet departments when pressed come up with a dozen interesting homework tasks in an hour. A good homework task can usually be used in many different contexts, and for many years. So just a dozen good homework tasks a year will go a long way. Good planning saves time. I know of a science department that gives each pupil a booklet containing homework tasks for the whole year, with the teacher simply having to say which homework is to be done on which night. It took time to produce the booklet, but then all the work was done, and the teachers had less to worry about. There are several primary schools that set a big project as homework lasting most of a term. Here, all the planning is apparently done by the pupils, but they generally enjoy the work as it is so much their own. Careful guidance on project topics means that this technique can play a vital strategic role in the curriculum. Whatever technique is used, homework-setting is always easier and more effective if planned in advance.

Some teachers only set homework because they have to. When a school comes up with a grand homework policy, teachers may feel they are being pushed to set homework when it is inappropriate. If you are thinking that way (unlikely, I guess, as you're reading a book on homework), I'd like you to consider what might happen if your department decides homework isn't necessary. You may justify this to your colleagues, your pupils, and the pupils' families. But then there are two things that might be done about the homework time you have 'released'. You could offer 20 or 30 minutes a week to another department that wants to set extra homework. A queue of pupils might then come to see you, demanding homework, on the grounds that some other horrible department is setting twice as much, and is blaming you. Alternatively, your Head and the timetabler might congratulate you for getting through the syllabus in less time than had been allocated (because the school had assumed you would need both class and homework time), and tells you that next year you'll have less class time, and could well have to make a member of staff redundant, as it would be an inefficient use of resources to 'teach' the whole syllabus and set none of it for homework. Failing to set homework should have such consequences, though I'm aware that many schools ignore these issues. Decisions on homework should properly be issues for the whole school.

What stops teachers setting homework is rarely, I think, a belief that it is genuinely pointless, but a dislike of the hassle involved in setting, monitoring and assessing it. What can help? Setting interesting homework will of course help inspire the pupils. Yet some homework is never going to be exciting. In that case, try hammocking. A hammock is a bed raised off the ground by two supporting trees. In television, a potentially unpopular programme may lose the channel many viewers. When a channel has to broadcast such a programme — perhaps a charity appeal (to impress the licensing authorities) or a party political broadcast — they will usually try to 'hammock' it. They put a strong programme before and after the unpopular one, hoping that the strength of the programmes on either side will raise its viewing figures high enough to keep the channel from going broke. Homework can be similarly hammocked. A strong lesson either side of an unpopular homework can 'hold it up', as long as the lessons really do support the homework. Think of the worst homework in the world and see if it can be hammocked. My worst homework (and the worst homework of many people who have been asked) is to learn a list of words. I was set this homework in several different subjects, sometimes foreign vocabulary, sometimes technical words, sometimes words I've misspelt. Hammocking can help. If the words are in another language, the first lesson might involve playing a record or an extract from a movie that included the words to be learnt; the homework, learn these words; the second lesson, play the record/movie again and translate it skilfully and enthusiastically. If the words are technical, perhaps in mathematics, the first lesson might involve looking at a 'silly' piece of writing that used no technical words (for example, 'Could I have a bar of that chocolate with three pointy bits at each end, because I've just come back from seeing a tall pointy thing in Egypt, and found that my parrot had just died'); the homework, learn the words 'triangle', 'pyramid', and 'polygon'; the second lesson, write a new version of the silly sentence, using the technical words. (Putting words into sentences is suggested again in Chapter 6.) If the words are spellings, and the class is kind and supportive, the first lesson could involve giving back a set of previous work, and listing the misspelt words (taken from all the work); the homework, learn the correct spellings; second lesson, correct each other's work (that's why you need a kind class), with points, credits, or prizes, for the most spellings corrected.

As well as hammocking, pupil involvement is important. Pupils could choose their own homework tasks, perhaps by having one big topic, with pupils choosing which section to study. This could improve motivation at the same time as reducing the work of the teacher. Pupils often say that an 'individualised' homework task is more inspiring, and there are ways of achieving this differentiation without extra work. Homework will also be improved if it connects one topic with another, or one subject to another: setting homework in 'broad' way, like this, makes use of the fact that, outside lessons, pupils rarely divide subjects quite as rigidly as the timetable suggests: pupils have, after all, spent several years in primary schools with far less rigid subject divisions. This may require teachers to co-operate more, which would be no bad thing. Pupils have told me that they would work harder on homework if they were writing more about their personal experiences, and if they thought their teachers really cared about their homework. I'm sure this is a little unfair on teachers, who try hard to make work personally relevant, and do indeed care, but the impression given to pupils may lag behind the impression intended by the teacher. Teachers can, anyway, fall into the trap that they think the pupils lack interest in homework so they need only set boring tasks. Being aware of the need to show that you care about homework is the lesson to be learnt.

Teachers who think pupils hate doing homework may think it absurd to set an upper time limit on a homework task. However, by setting such a limit, there should be less stress for those pupils who try to do homework well, and there may well be an incentive for pupils to do 'extra' homework, so as to appear especially 'clever' in apparently completing so much homework in such a short time. Timings are essential in organising good homework. Teachers would be shocked if told that their lesson should last 'as long as it takes', and that they may not feel the need to have any lessons one week, if the previous week's lessons were particularly good. Yet the same is all too often said of homework. Flexibility may be a good thing — and sound ideal for homework — but a constant, vigorous, complaint from pupils is that is is unfair to be given homework in 'lumps', with none for several weeks then all subjects in one week. This happens so often a couple of weeks into each term (week one: be kind; week two: set a big homework; week three: collect the homework), and two weeks before a holiday (better get a homework set before the last week of term, so I can mark it before the holiday). In practice, homework is not genuinely flexible, just lumpy. 'Flexibility' is too often used as an excuse for lack of planning. A rigid homework timetable may be disliked by teachers, resenting interference, but it can benefit pupils. It will help pupils to organise their work if teachers set realistically time-limited homework tasks within an overall limit — that is, minutes per week in every subject. A simple way to find out how long pupils take over homework is to get them to write the timing at the end of the work, or in the homework diary. Otherwise, teachers will only guess.

In the same way teachers may be unaware of how long a homework task will take. A routine homework might be 'find a description of medieval castles in an encyclopaedia, and copy it in your book'. I've watched a pupil in year 7 spend 20 minutes, in a Homework Centre, finding an encyclopaedia and an entry on castles, half an hour reading the article (and asking me about difficult words), and a further half hour copying out the most interesting bits. The resulting work — about half a page of writing — looked to me, as an experienced teacher, to have taken about 20 minutes. Yet in fact the pupil had spent 80 minutes of hard work on the task. It was only because I worked in the Homework Centre that I realised how long some homework tasks were. Should the homework have been stopped after 20 or 30 minutes? In some circumstances, yes, but I asked the pupil whether he had any other homework, and he said no. One long homework task seemed a reasonable alternative to the three short homework tasks that should have been set, according to the homework timetable.

When it comes to monitoring homework, this is easy if every pupil always does the homework, or if no pupil ever does the homework. For the rest of us, it is most important that homework gets monitored, so that there is a reason for the pupils who do homework to carry on doing it, and a reason for those who don't do homework to start. There are technical monitoring systems, tick lists and coded marks in registers, that can help, but it would be unwise to expect one system to fit all teachers in all schools. (My slightly nasty system involves putting a red box around the square in my mark book where a lax pupil would have got a mark, so that even if he or she hands the homework in the next day, and I don't get round to marking the work for another week, I will always know that it was late.) Better than promoting such systems, is to promote a principle: always make sure that you acknowledge homework done, or not done, during the lesson in which it should be handed in. This is particularly important if you are not going to mark the homework immediately. Lack of acknowledgement causes a huge amount of resentment. I've tried this exercise in an INSET session with experienced teachers. First I ask them to write down the three things they would most like to change about the National Curriculum, and justify these changes. When they've finished, after about 10 or 15 minutes, they give the papers to me. I immediately throw them in the bin. When challenged by the annoyed teachers, I say that what was important was that they did the work, and that what I think about the work, or whether I check it, is much less important. They disagree, quite rightly. Even as adults, we need our work to be acknowledged and responded to in some way. As school pupils, this is essential. I find it useful to separate the acknowledgement of work from a full assessment of it. Teachers can rarely mark work as quickly as they would like, and it is better to say to a pupil straight away 'that looks really good, I'll look forward to marking it properly', followed by a fortnight's delay before it is marked, than to ignore the work at the time, but mark it in a week.

Once a teacher has monitored the homework, and knows who has or hasn't done it, the question is what to do with the pupils who have failed to do the work. If the response is 'do it by tomorrow', then why should any pupil do it on time? Why not set tomorrow as the deadline? If the response is 'never mind', because they can't do much anyway, or you feel they come from an unsupportive family, then why make them come to school at all? How can you complain about an unsupportive family if the teacher, too, doesn't care whether or not the work is done? If the response is 'you will sit in the classroom at break, with your hands on your head' (or any other non-working punishment), then how is the pupil to understand what value you think the homework has? I would suggest these strategies.

- Always record failure to do homework, however good the excuse, so that there is some way of distinguishing the punctual from the lax or troubled.
- If possible, record the excuse, for posterity. Get an exercise book, and head each page with a pupil's name. Get a lax pupil to write their homework excuse in the book, with the date of the lapse. Such a book can give a teacher immense pleasure at Parents' Evenings, and pupils, I have found, understand the inappropriateness of even one example of

'I forgot'. (At the start of a course, I often ask the group what their favourite excuses are. My favourite is 'I was too upset to do the work, because I ran over a duck whilst cycling home from school'.) Recorded excuses can be the basis of negotiation at a later date; a teacher's raised eyebrow (the most common response to an excuse) rarely changes the world.

- Where a sanction or punishment is wanted, it should involve doing the missing work (or some equivalent work). If the homework is important, then it seems appropriate to punish a pupil by giving him or her a detention in which to complete the homework. The teacher will then have demonstrated that he or she values the completion of the work, rather than simply valuing obedience. Persistent lack of homework should be treated as a learning difficulty like any other, and could sensibly be referred to the special needs coordinator.

- Better than punishments, give rewards for brilliant homework. Too often, homework is treated as an educational sub-plot, rarely getting star billing. Whatever the system of rewards in the school, make sure some of the top awards go to pupils doing good homework, and, as good homework often involves the help or cooperation of families, make sure they know at home.

As well as setting good, or at least well-hammocked, homework, and monitoring it, there is still the question of assessing homework. Speed of assessment improves its effect, as does the balance of positive over negative comments. In general, teachers who take a fortnight to mark homework spend the same number of minutes or hours marking the homework as teachers who mark it within a day. The difference is when they spend the time, not how much time they spend: yet the effect of quick assessment is enormous. A common description of 'favourite teachers' includes reference to how quickly and carefully they marked work. A common description of 'bad teachers' includes slow marking. Similarly, teachers who start their comments on a homework with a list of faults, going on to a shortlist of good qualities, will depress and discourage a pupil far more than a teacher who starts with the positive comments, and writes the 'faults' as a list of targets for future work. What would you prefer in your Appraisal statement — a list of faults, or a list of good qualities plus targets?

It will be easier or quicker to assess homework if pupils assess their own or each other's work, with you checking their marking later. Homework can also be assessed by classwork, as when homework involves revising for a test, or preparing a presentation to the rest of the class. Assessment is also speeded up if you assess homework according to one, narrow, specific, criterion, such as an element from a National

Curriculum Attainment Target. Best of all, homework can be made an integral part of a larger piece of work — perhaps project work — so there is no need to assess it separately, as long as it is carefully monitored.

When assessing homework, it is important to be able to distinguish the availability of support, or blocks to learning, outside school that might affect it. For example, a homework involving collecting information from a local travel agent might be a real challenge for a pupil scared of being attacked in the street; a 'research' homework might be very easy for the same pupil, if he or she had lots of reference books at home. It isn't that I would recommend giving lower marks to the pupil with lots of support or facilities at home, but rather that, in the comments about the work, reference be made to some of these factors. 'I'm really impressed that you got out and found those brochures', or 'What a great set of books you must have at home, Dulon: thank the family from me!', might seem appropriate. A final point about assessment involves tact. Several parents will admit that they, rather than their children, do a lot of the homework. Where this is obvious, I would recommend being positive rather than punishing the pupil for cheating. A comment could be made like 'An excellent piece of work, Michael, full of information and very well written. If you wrote it all yourself, well done. If someone else wrote some of it, don't forget to tell them how good it is'. A more cynical teacher might say to the pupil, 'Great, Nyama, I must phone your mother and congratulate her on the standard of her work'. Do also remember that negative comments, or impossible tasks, harmful as they are for pupils, can also be harmful or even embarrassing for parents. A parent told me of the history homework set for her son. 'He was being asked to research questions when there were no books in the library on the subject and I didn't have the answer in any of my vast collection — I had just finished my History degree at the time and have been collecting history books for over 20 years! As a parent I was feeling very inadequate that I was unable to help.'

The following chapters will look at some ways of setting interesting homework, including examples of hammocking. They will look at ways of making homework more important: only if homework is important can it be justified. The chapters are divided into subjects or groups of subjects — a slightly arbitrary division, but one based on subjects having some common problems or advantages, when it comes to homework. Several subjects are simply ignored, such as Classical Languages and Civilisation, or Sociology, or form just a small part within another subject, such as Drama, Dance or Welsh. This is not meant as an insult. I've spent more time teaching and examining Sociology than anything else over the years, and think it a grand subject. My only criterion for including subjects was whether they were in the English National

Curriculum. There are enough homework suggestions here, I'm sure, that can be adapted to other subjects. In any case, the main purpose of the subject chapters is to open teachers' minds to some more of the possibilities of setting good homework: I don't imagine the lists of examples are comprehensive for any subject.

When thinking about homework tasks — as every chapter has several examples — I realised that there were some homework tasks that could be set in any subject. Here they are.

- Teachers who find themselves at the end of a lesson, with no idea what to set for homework, are liable to say 'I think we'll have a test next lesson: the homework is to revise for the test'. This is not unreasonable; at least if you are clear about what should be revised. With more preparation, a test can be given out in class, with the homework task to research the answers, and the test set 'officially' in the next lesson. A useful trick, whenever revision is set as homework, is to ask the pupils at the start of the next lesson whether they've done the homework: most, presumably, will say they have. Then, when you mark the tests and give them back to the class, you can say 'considering you all revised for the test, these marks are not as good as I had expected'. On such occasions, pupils have been known to insist on telling you that they *didn't* do any homework: a rarity, this.

- More interesting than setting a test yourself, you can ask the pupils to set a test. They are nearly always keen to think up questions for other people to answer, and a good homework would be to divide a topic up into sections, and get different pupils, or groups of pupils, to think up questions for each section. No one would then have an advantage in the resulting test. Ground rules are needed, so that questions are not impossible: perhaps saying that all the answers must be found in a certain book or set of books.

- Some tests can be done at home. A common way of recycling tests is to set a test once in class (following a revision homework), and to set the test again for homework. Many teachers set this 're-test' only for pupils who have low marks. This seems a little unfair on those pupils with high marks (who deserve homework, too), so perhaps the re-test could be for those pupils whose marks have gone down since the previous test.

- Similar to a test, but easier to set, is the alphabet game. Write the letters of the alphabet down the side of a piece of paper, and fill in words starting with each letter. This can be adapted to suit any subject from Art (names of artists, or art techniques or materials), to Zoology (names of animals), and has been used by Supply and Cover teachers for years. The advantage of setting such a simple task for homework is that pupils are encouraged to do research from books, from other pupils and from teachers and family. 'Tell us about some famous women in History, sir', I was asked by a pupil I had previously thought uninterested both in History and women. Later, I caught up with the news of a wonderfully simple and clearly inspiring competition, run for the whole school, asking pupils to list as many famous women as possible. Other simple letter and word games, adaptable to different subjects, include making anagrams of names or key words (my name becomes the cool and appropriate *just learnin'*), making up a sentence containing each of a list of key words (a game rather spoilt by its use in 1930s Europe to test for 'mental incapacity' and therefore suitability for extermination), or completing word searches (which can be generated by computers these days) or crosswords. All these games can be fun, and with planning can make a valuable contribution to the curriculum. It is easy, though, to set such tasks in a routine way, hoping that the fun will be justification enough. I would therefore use them with care.

- Following on from the principle that, for pupils, setting a test is often more educative and more inspiring than taking a test, why not get the pupils to take a lesson? Homework, in this context, can either be to prepare for such work, or, where the timetable allows it, to do such work. Pupils can do excellent work with younger pupils, either supporting the teacher or making a presentation. The experience of explaining work is often inspirational, and is certainly likely to increase the sympathy with which pupils regard their teachers. Work with younger pupils can be justified for all pupils. Those of considerable ability, who find their own work rather too easy, can be challenged by work that would otherwise be regarded as 'beneath them'. Those with learning difficulties can have a good 'excuse' to work on more basic tasks. Those with challenging behaviour are often the best at keeping order when teaching.

- A related homework is to ask pupils to prepare a presentation within their own class. I would especially recommend this when a series of lessons appears to be going nowhere. A student teacher who was very dismissive of the work of pupils in a series of my lessons he observed, was astonished when, in the 'presentation' lesson where pupils explained their work to the class and answered questions from other pupils, they were uniformly knowledgeable and articulate. (And, to be honest, I was surprised too.) The homework task would be to prepare for such a presentation. The stakes can be raised if the presentation is announced as being one that will be tape recorded. Oral work like this should also, at times, be very formally assessed, so that pupils realise that the spoken word is significant, just like written word.

- Following up the 'presentation' work, a second homework might be to write a report on what happened in the presentation lesson (either their own bit of the presentation, or the whole lesson), perhaps with the aim of making the reports into a display or permanent record of the presentation. This becomes a sort of double hammock, as the topic work, the presentation, and the display, are like three trees between which are slung two homework tasks.

- Assessment is such an important part of the work of teachers, it is as well to make it more significant for pupils. Whenever possible, pupils should be encouraged to assess themselves. In some ways, doing a self-assessment for homework can be risky: it is difficult enough being self-critical, without having to do it 'out of context'. However, there are many self-assessment tasks that make for good homework, and good independent learning in general. A homework might be set where pupils summarise all the work they have done that term, or make a hierarchical list of the most important things they have learned, or choose and copy out the single piece of work they would most like to be remembered for, to be kept in a portfolio of the class's best work. Analysis of work habits, with questions about where and when homework is done (and who or what interrupts it), can be useful for the whole school to know, as well as for the pupil. It is useful to get pupils to ask other people (such as family members or other teachers) what helps them work, or what aspects of a subject they most enjoyed, to be written up as a comparison with the pupil's own preferences. The pupils could also be asked to pair up, and do mutual assessments of each other's work. (This works well for teachers, too, and is preferable to a 'top down' style of Appraisal.) Simply talking about work habits and achievements, outside the classroom, is justification enough for such homework tasks. If pupils are given the relevant National Curriculum Attainment Targets to work from, they may even get a better grasp of assessment than their teachers!

- Many teachers feel they are unable to get their pupils to do enough homework because the pupils watch too much television. (An HMI survey done in the 1930s said much the same about the effects of radio.) One solution would be to set 'watch the television' as homework. It would help if the programme was relevant to the subject being taught, but imaginative teachers could probably find a task that could involve watching almost anything. Why might a Maths teacher ask pupils to watch 'Top of the Pops'? Perhaps to estimate favoured camera angles. Why might an RE teacher ask pupils to watch the FA Cup Final? Perhaps to analyse heroism, adulation and charismatic power.

- Surveys of various kinds have become very popular in recent years. Teachers, I guess, have so many forms to fill in themselves, that they have decided to make pupils understand the joys of tick lists. Surveys constructed by pupils are often full of leading questions, and the people they get to fill in the surveys often make appallingly unrepresentative samples. However, surveys do engage pupils, and can be used to enhance any subject. My favourite surveys are the ones that concentrate on engagement and don't pretend to be too rigorous. Pick a word (like 'revolution' in History), an object (like an apple in Food Technology), or a picture (like *Guernica* in Art); ask the pupils to ask a small number of adults what they think about the word, object or picture. Such a simple homework survey can be an ideal introduction to novel issues: it really can kick-start an otherwise daunting topic.

So, set, monitor, and assess homework well, and the pupils can learn more and be less stressed. The rest of this book looks at more detailed descriptions of homework and study support, according to subjects and forms of support.

CHAPTER 6

English

Could we abolish English homework? In one sense, of course we could. Yet every pupil in an English-speaking country, and just about every pupil in the rest of the world with access to films, television or pop music, will be doing English homework whether or not it is set. And before schooling starts, pupils will have done more language learning than any other 'subject'. Most pupils learn English from their families, not from professional teachers, and develop their skills doing other tasks, rather than in distinct lessons. It is English, then, of all school subjects (in English-speaking countries), that retains most of the qualities of the education available before schools became common. English teachers therefore use the universality of language — the fact that it will have been used by pupils throughout their lives and in all contexts — to enormous advantage. This chapter will look at some of these opportunities, all of which should also be applicable to those pupils with English as a second language. In Wales, Welsh is a part of the National Curriculum, and it follows two models. One is for those with Welsh as a first language, for which the homework suggestions for English, here, are most appropriate. The other is for those with Welsh as a second language, for which the homework suggestions in Chapter 9 are more appropriate.

The importance of English was never doubted, and was even enhanced, during the controversies around the setting up of the National Curriculum. There were controversies about the forms of English that should be taught, and about the literature that should be taught. Both controversies have implications for homework. On forms of English, there were arguments about whether one form of English, 'Standard' English (SE) should be taught to the exclusion of other forms. SE is useful to know, but should pupils be discouraged or prevented from using other forms in school? I don't want to be dogmatic in the debate, but as far as homework goes, if SE is insisted upon at all times, then the enormous advantage that English has for homework will be reduced. The talk and writing that pupils come across outside school will certainly not all be SE, so the possibility of 'engagement' with home and community will be reduced if pupils can only use one form of the language. Perhaps those promoting exclusive use of SE would like to make everyone, not just school pupils, use the same English, rather as the French promote a standard form of French. In that case, we all have plenty of homework to do! The other controversy, over literature, was concerned with whether there should be a stipulated 'canon' of texts, to be taught to all pupils. The effects on homework of the implementation of such a policy would also have been ambiguous. If there were a standard canon of literature, then parents might more easily support their children by buying the 'canon'; however, as with SE, most people are not reading canonical works every day, some never read them, so promoting a canon might sideline much interesting and valuable reading material.

For English homework, I recommend following certain principles.

• As pupils will come across so much English outside school, English homework should frequently engage with this wealth of source material. This may seem obvious, but most homework tasks (in every subject) are capable of being done in school, and therefore require no engagement at all. Most indeed are thought to be 'spoilt' by any interruption from family members or television. Yet the most popular Key Stage 1 homework is paired reading with family members, promoted in recent years by PACT and similar schemes. I'm told that as many children learn the alphabet whilst with adults watching Channel 4's 'Countdown', as learn it from children's or educational programmes. Secondary schools can profit from this habit of engagement.

• Written and spoken English have different 'weights' in and out of school. In school, despite wonderful improvements in oral work, pupils tend to think that talking is, in general, wrong, and that a lesson with no written outcome is not a real lesson. (Few teachers will say they believe this, but pupils report otherwise.) Outside school, however, talk wins out, the phone over the letter, the television over the book. Homework can profitably incorporate some of this 'significant speech', from outside school, just as it can promote beyond the school the practice of writing effectively for a variety of purposes.

• There are often regular, repeated, homework tasks, such as 'read a book for at least 10 minutes every day'. Like exercise routines, that also take 'only 10 minutes a day', it is all too easy to get out of the habit. The obvious 'monitors' are family members, who might record the reading in a homework diary. Standard reading homework tasks certainly need careful monitoring. And where a regular reading homework is to read parts of a set text, then it is also important that the reading makes a difference in the classroom. In some literature lessons, pupils are at no advantage if they have read the texts before the lesson: the homework is not hammocked. Obvious forms of hammocking would be to ask pupils to explain the text to other pupils, or answer questions about it. More subtle hammocking could be done by setting some sort of group activity, in which pupils will be pressured by their peers to do the homework or let the group down. If the monitoring and hammocking of regular reading tasks becomes a burden, it may be appropriate to turn the situation upside down, have regular silent reading sessions in class, with the homework task being to write up accounts of these. If appropriate, the class reading might be accompanied by carefully chosen music.

- All teachers are teachers of language. English homework should make use of the importance of the language to every subject. Now that curriculum maps and detailed schemes of work are available for most subjects in most schools, the English department can plan links. Those departments with whom links are made should become more aware of the significance of language, and their work should therefore pay dividends in the improved language skills of all pupils. There are obvious links with History — such as complementing the study of the 16th and 17th centuries with the words of Shakespeare, or complementing the study of World War One with war poetry. Less obvious and therefore more novel might be work on earthquakes to complement Geography (I read some wonderful letters sent between schoolchildren in London and Kobe after the latter's earthquake); work on Bible translations complementing RE (there are alternative translations in the *Oxford Anthology of English Literature*); work on news coverage of a planning dispute over a nuclear power station, complementing Science; creating glossaries of technical words for different sports, complementing PE. There is no reason for this to dominate all English teaching, but homework, where pupils can sit back and contemplate the meaning of life (sometimes called day dreaming), provides a fine opportunity for a bit of a holistic approach.

These are principles that apply to English homework in general. The following examples of homework tasks should illustrate some of the possibilities of setting exciting homework tasks that follow these principles, and that also follow the themes stressed in the National Curriculum. I should say here, as at the same point in each of these chapters, that I don't claim personal credit for thinking up all these tasks. The very best ones are mine, of course, but the rest, who knows?

- A simple phrase can be said in many different ways. 'I'm doing my homework now' could be said angrily, sadly, cheerfully, cynically, obsequiously, pompously, and so on. Set the homework task of practising saying this phrase in each of these ways. The homework can be well hammocked, as pupils enjoy coming up with other adverbs to add to the list you give them, and may enjoy hearing you trying to say the phrase in a couple of the ways yourself. In the follow-up lesson, the pupils can work in pairs to test out their skill at speaking in these ways, with the partner practising their listening skills by trying to guess the adverb being illustrated.

- Lists of adjectives, nouns, and verbs can be thought up, for homework, in preparation for a game of grammatical consequences in class, in which pupils consecutively write an adjective, adjective, noun, verb, adjective, adjective, and noun. Hence 'smelly hairy power-rangers laughing fast green buses'.

- What are the most common words (or the most common verbs, or the most common words with more than three syllables and so on) in use? Brainstorm for the ones pupils think are most common (presumably excluding offensive words), and write a list of the six favourites. For homework, get the pupils to listen carefully, for 30 minutes or an hour, to conversations (or television programmes, if the topic suits), and tick off the number of times each word is used. Feed back the results in the next lesson. Perhaps different groups of pupils could record conversations in different situations — some during mealtime, some when young people are talking amongst themselves, some in a shop, and so on.

- Someone once told me that since leaving school, the only thing they had read was a box of corn flakes. They may be surprised to learn that there are almost 1000 words on a corn flakes packet. As a homework, get pupils to read something that is not usually thought of as 'real' reading, to be reported on in the next lesson. Cereal packets could work well, as could all the words of shop signs in the local high street, or the printed words appearing in television advertisements (another surprisingly high total), or the signs or notices inside a car or bus. By making pupils read what they might otherwise fail to bother about, we can make them more aware of the uses of language and the different styles used in different contexts.

- Homework can be very difficult if the task has no structure. I used to hate 'open' writing tasks, and can still remember the fear of being set the homework 'write an essay, on any subject you want'. I'm sure others have different fears, but mine was lack of structure. An interesting way of creating structure was suggested by an English teacher who commented on working in a room after another teacher.

There was often a part of a poem left on the board, the ends of the lines hastily and inefficiently erased. The pupils were always more interested in the almost disappeared poem than in the work to be done in their own lesson. The teacher, therefore, took to writing a poem on the board himself, then half rubbing it out before the lesson started. When pupils said 'what is that about?', he could do a stunning lesson. A good homework writing task, based on the paradox of the interest inspired by the disappearing poem, would be to give pupils a poem or piece of prose with the ends of lines erased. The more 'real' the erasing the better. Perhaps a daring teacher could get some very old, used, exercise books from the back of some cupboard, and tear a few pages in two, vertically, with a homework task being to complete the work.

- Rules of language use are not always what they seem. Take being polite. Most people would say that there was a 'politeness' rule in their house, and that being more polite would be seen as a good quality. A simple experiment by the ethnomethodologist Harold Garfinkel involved his students going home and being 'polite', acting as though a visitor to the house. Almost universally, the students being 'polite' were insulted and otherwise told off by their families: doctors were called, rows were frequent. 'How dare you say that: people will think we don't feed you properly' was the angry response from a father to a son who said 'please could I get some food from the fridge?' I have not yet dared set such a task for homework, but a milder, less risky, version, would be to get pupils to change their 'normal' ways of speaking. (Do preface such a homework with a 'health warning', and an explanation of how to get out of the situation in emergencies, as Garfinkel's students had to.) Talk to your younger brother/sister as you would normally talk to your teacher (*not* vice versa); talk to a friend as though you'd never met them before. Record the results as soon as possible after trying such an experiment. The records should provoke lively debate in the next lesson.
- Pupils can transcribe real conversations, and can try to 'script' similar ones, as a way of studying the 'real' rules of language. They could (audio or video) tape an everyday conversation or an unscripted piece of talk on television, such as one of the confessional chat shows. Having been taught rules of transcription, preferably including marks for pauses but no added 'literary' punctuation, pupils could transcribe a couple of minutes of the conversation. When done properly, this is a fascinating exercise, and can certainly provide material for many good follow-up lessons. Pupils are often most impressed, after this exercise, that actors manage to make scripted dialogue sound so natural, when scripts are so different to transcripts of conversations. And the exercise is a good introduction to playwrights like Pinter or Beckett, who

suddenly make more sense. As a second homework, and a difficult one, pupils could write a dialogue with all the characteristics of transcribed conversation. Tom Leonard wrote a beautifully ironic poem about 'thi six a clock news', saying 'if / a toktabbot / thi trooth / lik wanna yoo / scruff yi / widny thingk / it wiz troo.' I believe that the comedian Frankie Howerd had every 'ooh' and 'ah' scripted, and his apparently stuttering delivery was all obsessively rehearsed. Should anyone have access to his scripts, I'm sure pupils could learn from them. Both transcribing and scripting, then, provide good homework tasks.

- Is a picture worth ten thousand words? Take photographs of the class at regular intervals. It would be a good idea to get a pupil or a visitor to the class to take the photographs, from a single position, perhaps every 2 minutes for 20 minutes. Copy the photographs and make a worksheet of them. For homework, get the pupils to describe in writing what was happening, maybe in the form of a 'photo-story'. How good to let families know what goes on in the classroom, too! In the subsequent lesson, get pupils to present extracts from their accounts. The photographs and the accounts based on them would, if sensitively edited, be ideal material for a Parents Evening or Open Day exhibition.

- Is a word worth ten thousand words? Pupils can find out for homework about the actual uses of words. Dictionaries, and references to an apparently rigid and unambiguous Standard English, can give the impression that language is fixed and knowable. Always a little pedantic, I bought the immense *Oxford English Dictionary* a few years ago, because I thought it would improve my accuracy. Instead, it made me realise the fluidity and uncertainty of the language: every word has been spelt and used in many ways, and a language that once appeared definite to me, now floated around like a rudderless boat. Pupils should know this, and can contribute to everyone's understanding of words by investigating them. What exactly does 'cool' mean (it has over 40 definitions in my *OED*), or 'good', or 'respect', or 'education', or 'stylish'? They can do a brief survey.

- Pupils can make their own dictionaries, for homework. A good task is to ask pupils to write explanations of words for younger pupils. I've set seven-word limits on definitions of even complex words, although you may wish to be a little more generous. By concentrating on words with which pupils are already familiar, the exercise can help pupils appreciate the difficulty of explanation; by concentrating on more difficult or technical words, the exercise can develop an improved vocabulary. A related exercise would be to get the pupils to make up new words, to match definitions you have given them: for example, a machine for measuring the level of brain activity in a classroom, the feeling you get when someone tells you a joke you've heard a hundred times, the noise made when you push a spoon through the seal on a new jar of instant coffee. The word 'quiz' is said (improbably) to have been invented as a result of a bet that the inventor couldn't introduce a new word into the language within a day, the bet being lost, as the word was scrawled on walls around Dublin overnight, and the next day had become a subject of conversation and lexicography. Could pupils come up with any inventions as good as this one?

- However ambiguous meanings can be, secondary age pupils expand their vocabularies by roughly 1000 words a year, sometimes increasing to 4000 or 5000 a year. That is at least 3 words a day, 20 a week. Every pupil to whom I've said this has been surprised, and has wanted to know what the 20 words were that they might have learnt in the last week. I would like to set a homework that simply asked the pupils to record any new words they learn during the week. The danger is that they will look out for technical words learned in lessons, whereas in fact many of the new words will be quite ordinary ones, and learned outside lessons. I have picked out the 20 words, some quite technical but most rather ordinary, used in this chapter, that would most probably be learned in the teenage years or later. They are 'abolish', 'universal', 'enhance', 'dogmatic', 'context', 'controversy', 'engagement', 'implementation', 'canon', 'oral', 'complement', 'hammock', 'cynically', 'obsequiously', 'pompously', 'adverb', 'syllable', 'context', 'vertically', and 'ethnomethodologist'. Setting a homework to discover words learnt, is particularly interesting as it inverts one of the most common and most disliked of all homework tasks: learning lists of words. A father is quoted by MacBeath and Turner, saying 'I am getting a mite scunnered wi' the words. I can see they have to do them but could they not make it a wee bit mair interesting wi' puzzles or crosswords. Dress it up, you know what I mean.' I hope you do understand him. Pupils learn words in many ways, and getting them to realise this, by trying to spot the new words learned, is more interesting than giving them a list to be memorised.

- Language history builds on this sense of development and change, and provides opportunities for exciting homework tasks. Pupils can work on the history of their own use of language. What words do they first remember saying, or what words do others remember them first saying? What has made them change the way they talk, or the languages or dialects they use? Many kinds of homework can be set, with the most obvious one being to get the pupil to ask people who have known them some time, how their language has changed. This is a particularly good area of work for a class in which some pupils speak English as a second or subsequent language. It is all too easy for pupils, or teachers, to think that people who make occasional mistakes in

English are poor linguists. Work on language histories makes it clear that where English has been learned after two or three other languages, the learner is likely to be an immensely skilled linguist.

- Another way of making a positive use of a multilingual classroom is to set 'story' homeworks. In the last century, collecting stories, and putting them down on paper, became a serious academic discipline, with the Grimms leading the field. Fieldwork makes good homework, and asking people outside school — especially older people — to recount stories is particularly pleasurable — whether these stories are entirely fictional or are tales of family history. Where pupils have access to stories in different languages, and from different countries, classwork based on such fieldwork can only be enhanced. Making story books, for use by other pupils, gives an incentive to collect good stories. Some schools have made imaginative use of stories in languages other than English, creating language resources to be used across the Borough.

- Creating plays — perhaps out of stories collected by pupils — provides opportunities for stimulating homework. Rehearsal is a popular homework in many ways, in English and in other subjects, as rehearsal involves a journey between a script or idea and a performance. It is a model of hammocking. Pupils may be willing to rehearse for hours to make a performance good, and will often take on many 'adult' characteristics, getting other pupils to work together, organising props, being, in these ways, in charge. Responsibility like this always helps homework, confounding the myth that pupils want simple, routine, homework.

- Another piece of creative work needs a brave teacher. Take a piece of your own creative writing, a poem perhaps, and give it to your pupils, uncredited. Set the homework task of analysing, interpreting, the poem: this should be done as homework to minimise the opportunity for pupils to ask about the poem and its author. Get the pupils to report back in the next lesson. The only teacher I know who had the courage to set this task found that pupils had come up with meanings and interpretations that had never occurred to him, the author. Once the author was revealed, the pupils were fascinated that they could ask him about the poem, and, more important, that their interpretations were significant whether or not the author had thought of them himself.

- There are many other ways of working on texts, of course. A task that always fascinated me was reading the first sentence or two of a book, trying to identify it, and working out what it was about and when it was written. Pupils can be asked to continue the story, or describe the genre. They could also be asked to write 'first sentences' themselves, perhaps to suit particular genres. Some of my favourite opening lines (in chronological order) are:

Nature (the Art whereby God hath made and governes the World) is by the *Art* of man, as in many other things, so in this also imitated, that it can make an Artificial Animal.

Although I am an old man, night is generally my time for walking.

Sherlock Holmes took his bottle from the corner of the mantelpiece, and his hypodermic syringe from its neat morocco case.

'And so they've killed our Ferdinand,' said the charwoman to Mr Šveyk, who had left military service years before, after having been finally certified by an Army Medical Board as an imbecile, and now lived by selling dogs – ugly, mongrel monstrosities whose pedigrees he forged.

Geoffrey's bad enough but I'm glad I wasn't married to Jesus.

The authors (in alphabetical order) are Alan Bennett, Conan Doyle, Dickens, Hašek, and Hobbes.

- Another way of getting pupils to read difficult texts, at home, is the simple exercise of choosing the three sentences, or lines, that they most and least enjoyed, justifying their choices.
- A final difficult reading and writing exercise is adapted from a letter to the *TES* of 29th March 1991:

Rxxl bxxks dxbxtx xs pxxntlxxs

Whxn wxll thx rxxl bxxks xrgxxmxnt xnd? Sxrxly xt mxst bx clxxr thxt chxldrxn usx a vxrxxty of strxtxgxxs tx rxxd prxnt xnd thxt xn xndxrstxndxng xf thx rxlxtxxnshxp bxtwxxn lxttxrs xnd sxxnd xs xnly xne xf thx strxtxgxxs.

It muts be fairly obvoius to aynone raeding thsi lettre that raedres draw on thier konwledeg of how lagnuaeg wroks, thier abitily to recgonise wrods on sihgt and theri capacity to ues contextaul cleus to enabel them to maek senes of what has goen befoer and perdict what is cmoing next.

if Kenne- Cl- and Ma- Tu- can re- th- let- they mu- agr- tha- a mix- appro- is nec-. If th- ar- no- abl- to re- thi- let- th- mu- be stu- or cra-.

Could pupils write in any of these styles?

CHAPTER 7

Maths and Science

Maths and Science have much in common, most obviously their concern with the measurement of quantities, but also their systematic approach to enquiry involving the testing of hypotheses. Both make great use of technical concepts and their application to inanimate objects or animate objects treated as 'things'. This 'thingyness' (or 'reification') has implications for people and societies, and Maths and Science teachers have, happily, increasingly stressed the social relevance of their subjects. At the same time, the subjects are also packed with 'pure' problems, equations and other formal symbolic puzzles, that require solving. There are a few principles, when it comes to setting homework, that both subjects have in common.

- I've already suggested that homework is likely to be more successful if it requires pupils to 'engage' with their homes or whatever environment is used for completing homework. This means that for Maths and Science, I would recommend putting a stress on 'applied' problems to be done at home. Nearly all the examples, below, are of this kind.
- When more 'pure' tasks are set, teachers are I'm sure well aware that pupils may get little help from home in solving these tasks. It is in these subjects, more than any other, that adults can be found claiming incompetence. (Interestingly, illiteracy still carries something of a stigma, but innumeracy can be shouted from the rooftops.) More than this, parents may be positively scared of these subjects, which in itself can make pupils unsure of themselves. There is a great need for differentiation (though not necessarily setting different tasks), and good support for the homework in the lesson before, and good follow-up in the lesson after, the homework: hammocking, again. Really difficult homework tasks should at least be followed-up with a discussion of the difficulties in class. A positive way of building up the confidence of pupils is to get them to help, and assess, younger pupils.

- It is easy to underestimate the language skills needed for success in Maths and Science. This is, I know, more often underestimated by teachers of other subjects, and those who set exam papers (I'm told), than by Maths and Science teachers themselves. Nevertheless, it is worth stressing here the need to set homework in such a way that pupils skilled in the technical aspects of the subjects are not systematically disadvantaged by the language used in the setting of the tasks. Language is certainly worthy of homework in itself — especially learning and applying technical concepts — but teachers need to know when the biggest problem they set is linguistic and when it is mathematical or scientific.

- Showing workings is required of both subjects, just as preparatory sketching is required of much Artwork and re-drafting is required of much English work. Nevertheless, pupils and parents are often puzzled that they can get low marks despite a right answer. Teachers need to repeat the reasons for showing workings, as often as possible. Metaphors are useful: an answer without workings is like the body of a car without an engine. Or asking for an answer without the working is like asking for a return ticket at a railway station ('Where to, sir?' 'Here, of course'): it's the journey that's as important as the final destination.

- By dealing with the infinite, both subjects encourage a sense of awe and wonder. This sense is an important link with Religious Education teaching, and can help with homework. Pupils making 'incredible' discoveries are likely to be more enthusiastic than those endlessly repeating routine tasks.

Examples of homework tasks are separated into Maths and Science: the subjects are different, after all. A Czech joke tells of a Physicist, Biologist and Mathematician watching an empty house. They see two people go in; later, they see three people come out. The Physicist says 'there must be a problem with the measurement'; the Biologist says 'they must have reproduced'; the Mathematician says 'if one person goes into the house now, there will be exactly no one there'. Not a very funny joke, but how many are there that justify separating Maths and Science?

Maths

When I've worked in homework clubs — after-school sessions in which pupils can do homework and get some help from a teacher — the most striking thing I learned was that pupils enjoy completing homework. The second most striking thing I learned was that individualised Maths schemes (such as SMILE) were wonderfully supportive for homework.

Such schemes are sometimes criticised for their lack of whole class teaching, and the difficulty of listing the skills that all pupils will have been taught in each week, term and year. (Critics should be reminded that whole-class Maths *teaching* doesn't necessarily result in whole class *learning*.) However, when it comes to homework, individualised schemes are automatically differentiated, and pupils enjoy doing challenging tasks that are still within their grasp. Whether using an individualised or a more conventional curriculum, it is worth noting that Maths homework can be enjoyable and challenging, and that it has long outgrown the stereotype of routine, repetitive exercises. Here are some ideas for 'engaging' homework tasks.

- To engage with pupils' homes, there are many tasks that help pupils get a sense of building-based numbers. Simply getting pupils looking around their homes, as part of homework, will increase the chances of it being done. Calculations could be of the form 'multiply the number of windows by the number of doors, then divide by the number of rooms', or 'find and sketch examples from your home of angles of 90°, 60°, 45° and so on'.
- More complex house-based work would be the calculation of the proportions of rooms, or average floor space, to be analysed in class, perhaps, looking at the patterns of room function and room proportions or floor area. (Care must be taken to avoid embarrassing pupils coming from very small or very large houses: answers that don't 'give away' evidence of wealth or poverty are to be preferred.) More investigative work could be done on roof angles, making use of pictures of buildings in cold and hot countries, with useful links to Geography. Why are walls generally vertical, and flat rather than curved? Why are castle walls often curved? Why are windows generally set high up in walls?
- In recent years, many lessons have been given on lotteries, to exploit pupils' interest. I'm a little uncomfortable promoting a lottery for which pupils are mostly too young to buy tickets. However, there are just too many opportunities to be missed for good work on probability. I like working on some of the common mathematical misunderstandings. How do people choose their numbers, and are choices based on beliefs that certain numbers, or combinations of numbers, are more or less likely to be chosen? Who would be prepared to buy a ticket every week with the same numbers as the previous week's winning numbers, or with six consecutive numbers? Pupils can do useful survey work on such issues, with much follow-up work on the results of the surveys as well as their own beliefs about the lottery. They could simply work out how to spend £9 million, using accurate prices from catalogues and advertisements: their results would make a wonderful display.

- By surveying, pupils are of course engaging with people. Maths homework that engages with people can promote a better understanding of the subject well beyond the school population. Shopping exercises have always been popular, and homework could be set asking pupils to act as mathematical advisers to friends or families. Surveys of prices, involving work on 'average' shopping baskets, or work on petrol prices, including the value of the 'gifts' offered, could be useful. Why shouldn't pupils provide a consumer advice service to others in the school? A good link with Food Technology and Business Studies too.

- A teacher working on direct and inverse proportions might ask pupils to find, at home and beyond, examples of these interesting relationships. I once asked my pupils to do a survey, over the Christmas holiday, of the apparent happiness of people in their house at regular intervals for three days. I hesitate to recommend this homework, as I was upset to hear so many tales of rows and unhappiness, but the work on proportions was valuable. Levels of happiness were, in this study, inversely proportional to the number of men present. Less traumatic discoveries might be investigated: what is the relationship between food consumption and age, or between gender and preferences for television programmes, or voting behaviour of parents and children, or height and shoe size? Pupils could be set tasks to calculate the relevant proportions, or could be asked to discover and quantify unlikely proportions of their own.

- The interpretation of graphs is important in Maths and also a great contribution to other subjects. Pupils may feel keener to interpret graphs if the graphs are of the relationship between exam results at GCSE and A Level. There are now good exam statistics available from the ALIS and YELLIS systems at Newcastle, showing probabilities of gaining particular results. Homework could involve plotting their own most probable results, and (I would hope) planning how to improve on the predictions: 'target-busting', as it is called in the trade. Similarly relevant graph analysis, suited to homework, might include the use of income and health, or life style and life expectancy, graphs. I've set 'calculate your life expectancy, using these figures', as an RE homework, but I'd be happy to hand it over to mathematicians. Like the analysis of exam results, such work should not be allowed to encourage fatalism. Try target-busting again.

- The IMPACT scheme has published books of mathematical holiday games, targeted at key stages 1 and 2. Secondary Maths teachers might do well to adapt some of these games, or, better still, get the pupils to invent games for younger pupils or siblings. For example, spotting number plates whose numbers are divisible by 3, or 7 (an IMPACT game). An interesting piece of speculation that could help take your mind off a long holiday journey would be to consider a point on the surface of a wheel. A car or train travelling at 70 mph, and not (let us hope) skidding, would mean a point on the surface of the wheel stops, accelerates to 140 mph, and stops again several times a second, with each rotation of the wheel. There must be a good homework task based on this astonishingly rapid acceleration and deceleration. Mathematical board games and card games can also be produced by pupils, including tasks at all levels.

- Special games or puzzles can be good as occasional homework tasks. I've tried hard tasks, such as using exactly three 3s and mathematical symbols to generate every number from 0 to 10. Three 3s could be replaced by four 4s, too. Easier would be to ask them to think of 25 questions with answers of 100. As I've said in Chapter 5, pupils could be asked to think up puzzles themselves.

- Numbers are interesting in themselves. I've seen a wonderful, simple, History-and-Maths class task, in which A3 papers covered in dots, were laid out on the floor of the school hall. There were 6 000 000 dots, and the pupils were learning about the Holocaust. I've never seen such a good way of teaching a single number. In a large school, of 1000 pupils, every pupil in the school could be asked to do a Maths homework of producing 6000 dots (it takes about half an hour, by hand), so that their own dots could be put together for the Holocaust lesson.

- Other big number homework tasks could be estimating the number of bricks used to build the school, or the town, or all the buildings in the world; or estimate the world's population if no one had died in the last 100 years. Smaller numbers like *pi* might stimulate a mnemonic competition, starting from
I wish I could recollect of circle round
The exact relation Archimede found.

- Chaos theory has become fashionable, and the name itself is strangely attractive for teachers. Drawing a cloud, or working out how to measure a coastline, seems an easy homework task until you've studied chaos theory and worked on iteration and fractals.

- Maps and other scale drawings can be set as homework tasks, and link well with Geography and Art work. Maps of journeys to and from school, and scale drawings of objects or pictures found in the home, are generally engaging.

- Geometry and Business Studies can be combined. A good homework task I've seen involves preparation for a class role-play on a 'baked beans war', with pupils competing to design optimum baked beans cans.

- A pupil once said to me, sympathetically, 'it must be awful watching the television in your house: you're always thinking about what's on and what it all means'. Awful indeed. I mentioned in Chapter 5 a possible Maths homework, calculating the different camera angles used in 'Top of the Pops'. How about working out the mean age of characters in different soap operas, as some are 'older' than others? Or the modal number of 'cuts' in a 30-second advert? Simple tasks such as noting down programmes, or phrases within programmes, containing numbers or other mathematical terms. This could become a game of spotting shapes: for example, which pupil can be the first to spot a hexagon on the television. The same sort of spotting games have also been used with newspapers and magazines, and these, more easily than television programmes, can be brought into school.

Science

Research on Science teaching discovered a paradox: pupils often came out of Science lessons with a more confused and inaccurate picture of the world than they had when they went in. 'Thinking Science', now rightly fashionable, is a way of approaching Science teaching that seeks to focus on how pupils develop their concepts and models of the world. The Nuffield approach to Science has had this exploratory, pupil-centred, approach for several years now. When setting homework, Science teachers of whatever school or theory, need inevitably to think of how pupils can tackle problems on their own. For homework, Thinking Science is particularly recommended. Pupils *are* scientists, in this model, and are not just learning about Science. They can talk informally as well as formally about their Science topics when working outside the classroom, and this flexibility should help when they come back to class.

The obvious limitations when it comes to Science homework is the lack of laboratories and technical apparatus at home. Some teachers take this as a cue to set every homework as 'write up your classwork'. Writing up classwork can indeed be done at home, but it can hardly be expected to inspire pupils every week. Treating houses as arenas for 'field experiments', and getting pupils to 'think' at home, are the two approaches most used in the recommended homework tasks described here. I've not attempted to match tasks to year groups or ATs, but have grouped them into three themes — the home as laboratory, the world as laboratory, and the brain as laboratory ('pure' thinking). More or less sophisticated versions of each task could be written for different year groups.

- Home as laboratory.

The house is full of measurement scales: degrees on ovens and central heating systems, energy on food packets, frequency on radios. Do a survey of all the measurement scales used in your home, with a prize for the most, or the most unusual (a flood-level post, marked in fathoms?).

Experiment on yourself. Test your pulse on the hour every hour for 12 hours, listing (with appropriate propriety) what you were doing at each time. Or test for reaction time, using the 'dropped ruler' technique — and therefore involving someone else in the home. Perhaps test the reaction times of people of different ages.

Make a hot drink — coffee or tea — and carefully time and estimate the heat changes and transfers, including the cooling of the liquid, heating and cooling of the mug and spoon, warming of the surface on which the mug is standing, and so on. More accurate measurements could then be done in a school laboratory. Related work on heat insulation could be done on, for example thermos flasks or pizza boxes. In the winter, survey the lagging in the house, and estimate which pipes might burst and why. (The pupils might also estimate the average call-out charge for a plumber, but that would count as Personal and Social Education (PSE), not Science.) Similar survey work could be done, for example on energy use, draughts or food types. Other house surveys might be of house plants, or mini-beasts in and around the house, or pets in the house and neighbourhood. Materials surveys, on the uses of plastics, or wood, or whatever, can also be done. More unusual, and interesting, might be a survey of sounds: homes are noisy places, filled with the sounds of (for example) road traffic, aircraft, neighbours talking, television and radio, bird song, heating systems, creaking floorboards, lifts, wind, kettles, and all the sounds made by people and pets.

An extension of the lagging homework: a safety audit of the home, and perhaps of the school as well. A safety audit of the school could also engage the premises staff, who are likely to be the experts on the whole topic. Like the previous homework, the benefits of doing well in this homework are considerable. I would caution against a high moral tone: 'You really should tell your family to get the whole flat re-wired' might not endear you to family or pupil.

I've seen homework tasks, relating to genetics, asking pupils to describe family similarities. If this is done, it should be done with considerable sensitivity, as most families get their genes from all over the place, with inheritance through generations of monogamous nuclear families being the exception rather than the rule. Another interesting PSE homework, then.

- World as laboratory.

Extending beyond the home, pupils could do environmental surveys of their immediate neighbourhoods, or surveys of the sky at night — a fascinating topic for homework. 'Reconstructing' the local environment, or the sky, in class, is the obvious follow-up to such exercises, including displays of pictures or diagrams done by different pupils or, if you're feeling adventurous, a role-play.

An interesting exercise, related to Biology and Physics, is to collect material for and build a bird's nest. I heard of this being set for a Year 4 class in Primary school — though there, parents/carers must have done a lot of the work.

Ecological issues are popular and motivate many pupils. On the basis of surveys and research work, pupils might produce an Ecology journal as a collective homework task, telling others of the issues they feel are important. This would also provide an ideal opportunity to differentiate tasks, according to the abilities and interests of pupils.

Book-based investigative work can easily be done, such as surveys of scientists, perhaps searching out women scientists.

Finding out the history of the measurement of time provides good cross curricular work with History, as the uneven length of months is related to arguments concerning Julius Caesar (July) and Augustus Caesar (August), with the arguments settled by giving August one of February's days. Equally complex histories can be found of the length of years, the numbering of years, the length of hours, the establishment of Greenwich Mean rather than local time (with the growth of railways), and so on. Pupils can be asked to speculate and/or do book research, if books are scarce or inaccessible.

Book research could well include reading some of the significant Science books — Darwin's *Origin of Species* would be as good a start as any, and books by Stephen Jay Gould or Richard Dawkins would develop the biological theme. Rom Harré's *Great Scientific Experiments* has a wider range of sources, and journal articles could also be used.

- Brain as laboratory.

Simple thought exercises might involve mnemonics (the bane of medical students), creating glossaries of key terms, or thinking of questions to test other pupils, as suggested elsewhere in this book.

Why's and what if's are popular; I feel they work better if pupils are not allowed to look up books. Why do animals huddle? Why do both eyes blink at the same time (a real evolutionary puzzle, this one)? As sliding down a stair bannister is so much easier than climbing up one, why is it just as hard walking down stairs as climbing up them? Why do people have eyebrows? Why are cartoon characters so often drawn with big heads? Why does a pencil, waved up and down in front of a television, 'flash', and flash more quickly when going up than down? What if we didn't have elbows (the title of a recent book for children)? What if gravity were reduced? What if you only had food to the value of 300 calories a day (the common diet in concentration camps)? What if the world's temperature increased by two or three degrees? What if H_2O became consistently more dense as its temperature lowered — that is, what if ice didn't float?

More complex 'thinking' problems could be on the work done by Superman — how much energy would it take to stop a speeding train with your hands, while standing on the sleepers, or what temperature would your breath have to be to 'freeze' a villain? For work on inheritance and natural/unnatural selection, 'design' a new breed of dog, for a particular purpose, taking characteristics of current breeds. How could you weigh a house, or a cloud? Given your knowledge of physiology, what might it feel like to be executed in different ways? (Gory, I know, but useful for debates on capital punishment, and always popular with pupils. There was a *New Scientist* article on the subject, but I won't give away its 'recommendations'.) There are so many scientific puzzles, and so many books of them, that teachers could easily set regular puzzle homework tasks, where the answers to the puzzle related to work done, or work about to be done.

CHAPTER 8

History, Geography and Religious Education

These three subjects, sometimes grouped as 'Humanities', are concerned with individuals and groups of people, societies, and the way they deal with the world. History looks at changes over time, and the forms of evidence for such changes; Geography looks at the inter-relationship between people and their environments, including the study of the physical environment itself; Religious Education looks at systems of belief that attempt to answer questions about people and the world. All incorporate controversy, or different perspectives on the world, whether these are about the significance of suffragism, the conflicts of interest over energy policy, or the events that follow bodily death. They all, also, were controversial in the way they became part of the National Curriculum. History, like English, was hotly and publicly debated. The debate surrounded issues such as the balance between British and World History, or factual knowledge and skills in the use of evidence. Religious Education (RE), whose status is still peculiar, having a locally not centrally determined syllabus, was the subject of debates about the balance between Christianity and other religions. Geography kept a much lower profile, with few widely publicised debates, yet the syllabus was changed, as a result of the Dearing Report, more radically, perhaps, than any other syllabus. It is the 'social' nature of these subjects, and their ability to incorporate, as well as provoke, controversy, that make all three particularly open to engaging and thoughtful homework tasks. Some principles apply to them all.

- Homework can, in these subjects more than any other, get pupils to talk to family, friends, peers, neighbours and anyone else they come into contact with. I've heard some teachers say 'parents equal trouble', when it comes to RE, or 'our job is to get the pupils to forget the prejudices of their families', when it comes to History, or 'migration is too sensitive an issue in this area, so we'll only study migration in the USA'. Yet family views don't go away if we ignore them: pupils simply learn two ways of thinking about the world, one way for school, another for home. In any case, insulting parents always rebounds, so that parents and now even governments become just as likely to say that 'teachers equal trouble' or 'our job is to get children to forget the prejudices of their teachers'.

- Teachers often, rightly, complain that it is difficult to resource homework, especially when pupils are unable to take books home. However, with Humanities subjects, resources are people (as in the previous point) and the social and environmental conditions in which they live. When planning homework, therefore, it may be best to start with the resources that are available to pupils, and work back from them.
- There are plenty of opportunities for extended project work here, with investigative work central to History and Geography (like Science and Technology, too), and in-depth understanding of people and their circumstances central to all the Humanities (like English).
- Extended writing is also expected, including 'essays'. Pupils often find essays difficult, because of the difficulty of planning and structuring them. One technique I've used is to give pupils opening sentences for each paragraph of an essay, allowing them to use these sentences or their own. This has proved particularly useful for pupils who prefer very short, structured exercises. Extended *speaking* shouldn't be underestimated, and pupils often enjoy this, finding it less stressful than writing for homework, even if the 'speech' in class is itself stressful.
- Pupils may be expected to read a lot for Humanities subjects. Amongst this reading should be stories and longer novels. There are published lists of relevant books, but teachers could do their own search of the library and English rooms. There are, similarly, songs of relevance to these subjects — though geographical songs are a little harder to come by that historical or religious ones. ('River deep, mountain high' is a little unspecific, and 'It's raining men' is positively confusing.)

History

Homework tasks promoting a better sense of chronology are a little illusive. Teachers of History are always sensitive to chronology, but sometimes think of it as being taught 'incidentally', whilst pupils learn about events and dates. Pupils, however, often find it difficult to gain a sense of the passage of time through History, and the ways in which 'periods' of History are defined.

- There are several timeline activities, in class and for homework, that can be done for any History topic, and will benefit from being done for all History topics. Having a detailed timeline, at the start of every topic, helps pupils have an overview of the topic, and can be used to check information throughout the topic. A simple homework activity would be for each pupil to choose (or have chosen for them) a single date and event from the timeline, and produce a small 'poster' of that date. These posters can then be put together into an attractive and very useful class display. Pupils could be asked to research their date/event, so that the poster has more information on it than is on the complete timeline.

- Periods may be described in terms of a single characteristic (such as feudalism, or rule by a particular dynasty), but are more often described in terms of a set of events or changes. These sets can be made into mnemonics by teachers, and learned or described or illustrated for homework. Or teachers could give pupils outline descriptions of periods, and get the pupils to create their own mnemonic. SEWCLAWUCCA, for example, could cover the 20th century (Suffrage, Empires, World War One, Communism, League of Nations, Abyssinia, World War Two, United Nations, Cold War, Computers, Aids).

- Key events can be described in class, and given in a jumbled form, for homework, to be re-ordered by the pupils. This can be quite a simple task, if pupils know a lot about the events, but I've seen tasks in this format that require sophisticated historical and logical skills. Some textbooks provide pictures in the form of strip cartoons that, once re-ordered, form the basis of extended writing. The Bayeux Tapestry is one such ready-made 'strip cartoon'.

- Quite open tasks, such as 'find events that happened in Europe in each of the years from 1830 to 1850', can help pupils get a better sense of the complexity of History, especially if they then compare lists in class, trying to decide which events are most significant.

History teachers may have less difficulty thinking of ways of setting homework that develops their pupils' range and depth of historical knowledge and understanding. There is a danger, however, of being too willing to set 'research' tasks that encourage pupils to copy out large chunks of encyclopaedias or textbooks, without thinking about what they are doing. Not all pupils will have easy access to relevant books, anyway.

- Where simple 'go away and research' tasks are set, it may be worth doing them as holiday or long-term homework tasks, and asking about 'peculiar' topics, on which there is unlikely to be a straightforward bit of copying that can be done. 'Find the history of football' would be more of a challenge than 'find the life story of Churchill'.

- Understanding often comes with comparison, and work for homework is often helpful when it involves comparing the history being studied to a familiar aspect of the pupils' lives. For example, follow work on the myths of the foundation of Rome with a homework asking pupils to make up legends on the foundation of their home town, or to make up another twins legend. Similarly, after working on the good and bad qualities of Louis XVI and/or Marie Antoinette as leaders, get the pupils, as a homework, to do a similar list of the good and bad qualities of a recent or current British Prime Minister as a leader.

- Where a lot of information is to be absorbed, homework could involve preparation for a demanding class activity. For example, give out information about different Medieval weapons, with their names and brief descriptions of how they work and what they are for. Get the pupils to learn them. In the next lesson, the pupils can be given several 'scenes' — for example, 'I am outside my enemy's castle, and there are people firing arrows at me; what weapon would be most useful to me, and why?' or 'I want to defend my city against invaders on horseback; what would be the weapon I would use the most, and why?'. They would have to 'solve' each scene as effectively as possible, and justify their choice to the rest of the group.

- Group work is a way of covering a lot of information in a short time, but it is also a way of getting pupils to put together their new-found knowledge and understanding. A class studying 18th century France might be divided, and asked for homework to research either the Monarch, the First Estate, the Second Estate, or the Third Estate. The homework could be to find information, or to use the information gathered in class to speculate on what their group's lives would have been like at the start of the revolution. In the next lesson, the class would be rearranged into groups of four, with one Monarch and one member of each Estate in each group. They would then have to use the information found out or learnt for homework to write a short scene or playlet about a meeting between these four people in Paris in 1789. A similar task could be set up, with pupils preparing for a role play about a tribunal hearing during World War One.

- Activities that can seem rather low level, might bring out considerable knowledge or understanding, if set up in the right way. Drawing a recruiting poster, for use during the mid-17th century, could require complex language skills and sophisticated historical skills.

I would say that interpretations of History are as numerous as historians, yet much History teaching either ignores the variety of interpretations or positively denies their existence. Whatever your position on that debate, the National Curriculum stresses the need to acquaint pupils with differing interpretations of the same event, and such work, whatever its historical value, is immensely valuable for the personal development of pupils.

- I'll start with a real bit of PSE, that may also help pupils understand and describe their own interpretations of events. Leaders are often seen as mysterious and almost superhuman. After studying any powerful leader, I've sometimes set the homework, on a prepared worksheet, of composing a letter to and from an 'agony aunt' (whose name can be chosen to amuse, if you enjoy that kind of joke). The leader's letter begins 'Dear ... I'm having a lot of troubles: no one seems to like me, and being a leader has caused so many problems, such as ...'. The agony aunt's letter begins 'Dear X, This is what I'd recommend ...' Good candidates from Britain include William I, Henry VIII, Elizabeth I, Cromwell, George III, or Lloyd George. Whether it is appropriate to include current figures, troubled or not, I'll leave up to you.
- Pupils can also write imagined dialogues between other characters, such as an invader and a member of the indigenous population, or a defender or critic of Charles I.
- Work on bias and propaganda can come under this heading, too. After classwork on bias, for example, on the character of Richard III, the Gunpowder Plot, or the Suffragettes, ask the pupils to cut out or video a news report that they think is biased, to be described to the class in the next lesson. The same could be done, of course, on the topic of propaganda — an issue too easily confused with bias. If pupils can't find examples of bias or propaganda in their everyday lives, they can't have learnt much from your lessons. And if you teach them to recognise and understand both, you will have done them proud.
- Preparing arguments for and against the abolition of slavery, as a homework task, can get pupils to understand that issues we now find easy to take a position on, were once hotly debated. (Perhaps the continued existence of an Anti-Slavery Society should warn me that the issue is still controversial.) It is important to give pupils enough information for them to make a good job of the arguments on both sides, without anachronism. All such work is related to work on current interpretations of those issues. Similar work could be done on the different positions taken over Charles I, or joining the First World War.
- Oral/aural homework. As part of the introduction to a large 'Revolutions' topic, including the Industrial Revolution and the French Revolution, ask the pupils to ask five adults what they understand by the word 'revolution'. The next lesson should start with a brainstorm of all the answers, to be used, for example, to categorise different types of revolution (e.g. social, political, technological), different qualities of

revolutions (e.g. disruptive, exciting, progressive, violent), and different attitudes to revolutions (positive and negative). It may also allow for discussion of the complexity of concepts, different perspectives on history and levels of understanding amongst adults.

History teaching requires dealing with many kinds of sources and questions, and enquiry skills can be the basis of good homework tasks.

- A popular Primary school homework, also useful for Secondary History, is bringing an object from home. The use of artefacts as historical sources is given more significance if pupils have brought objects and talked to the class about their use as evidence, having written about this for homework.
- Longer-term homework tasks might involve visiting a museum and reporting back on it. Similar work could be to describe a street or house, and such work would have the advantage of demonstrating to pupils that museums are not the only places to find historical artefacts. Or get pupils to find a war memorial. Where is it, and what does the inscription say?
- Questions can be asked of historical figures, especially if History teachers are willing to do a bit of acting. Ask your pupils, for homework, to imagine it is the evening of 27th July 1794. 'You have been allowed to interview Robespierre on the eve of his execution. He has agreed to answer three questions about his life, his beliefs, and so on. Work out what three questions you could ask him that would best help answer the question 'was he a hero or a villain?' It would be worth trying out a few (bad and good) questions in class first. For example, 'Are you a hero or villain?' could receive the unhelpful answer 'A hero'; 'Why do people want to execute you?' might get a better answer. In the lesson after the homework, the teacher role-playing Robespierre, could be asked the questions groups of pupils have decided are the best. Of course, real questions can be asked of real people, and a regular homework, with all the characteristics of engagement that I recommend, could be to interview people who have lived through significant periods or events. Older people are likely to have more to talk about, but young people live through important events, too, and there's no reason why pupils shouldn't interview fellow pupils.
- Problem solving is a related skill. What problems would the Romans have had in invading Britain? How could they solve them? Or what ways can you think up of negotiating between Native Americans and settlers in the 19th century? What about the Italians early in the two World Wars? Homework can engage pupils in speculation on such issues, and, assuming they follow class work on the topics, they require

no more than a pen, paper and brain. An extended piece of problem solving would be to put together ideas on preventing the Black Death in the 14th century, and for homework, get pupils to prepare for a 'discussion' on what the villagers should do and why.

Pupils must organise and communicate their knowledge and understanding. Homework seems an appropriate opportunity to practice extended narrative work, if the homework is sufficiently structured and supported.

- Project work is often used in History, and I've written separately about supporting project work. For History, I'd also promote the idea of homework as a way of getting pupils to prepare for oral assessments, or question and answer sessions, on projects.
- Letters home from and to the trenches are always popular with teachers. Pupils may also enjoy making the letters look old, for a display, though I'm not sure about the Health and Safety implications of oven-baking your homework. I've found it useful to set a series of homework tasks, interspersed with other tasks, so that pupils create a set of three or four pairs of letters, from and to different war arenas, and at different stages of the war. The pupils often get more and more historically sophisticated as the series goes on: this is likely to depend on the quality of the response to each set of letters as it is handed in! A series of letters can itself become an extended historical narrative, and other related work might include letters to newspapers, trying to stop the war at an early stage, or a letter from the Kaiser, asking for clemency after the war.
- After working on the diary of Anne Frank, get the pupils to write their own diaries for a week, and then, in supportive groups in class, analyse the validity and bias in the pupils' diaries, as a way of assessing the use of diaries by Historians.
- Whatever topic has been taught, a late homework task, prior to a self-assessment exercise, could always be to 'communicate knowledge and understanding' for future pupils studying the same topic. Such guides, written by and for pupils, can sometimes be, embarrassingly, better than guides produced by teachers.

Geography

Geographical skills permeate all work, yet some homework tasks can support specific skills. For example, creating maps and plans, whether of routes between home and school, or of imaginary desert islands, can develop pupils' geographical and creative skills. Work on 'places' too, of course, can be done in conjunction with any of the geographical themes, yet there are some surprisingly simple homework tasks that can inspire pupils. During a popular international event, such as the Olympics or World Cup, get the pupils to watch the events (not usually difficult!), and find out at least two facts about each country competing. They would need to have an atlas or encyclopaedia handy, although some information may be given in the commentaries. A large display of this information, related to the event, could provide geographical education for the whole school. Pupils know and visit places themselves, too, and reporting on places visited can be a good way of bringing the class together. In Chapter 26, I've described ways in which holidays can provide effective learning opportunities, and, especially if a pupil takes a holiday in term time, it seems reasonable to ask them to make the holiday more interesting by doing such work. It could, I suppose, be described as investigative work, but more systematic investigations need to be done through the course. Geographical issues are always in the news, and regular homework exercises following up and reporting back on important events can give pupils a greater sense of the urgency of Geography, and can, like the simpler 'looking up' tasks produce impressive displays.

Some kinds of fieldwork could be done as homework, and this has become popular in GCSE courses, where pupils may need less supervision. However, simpler investigations, not needing such active fieldwork, might include a summative piece of work, towards the end of a topic. For example, pupils, having studied Japan, could be asked to produce a set of solutions to one of Japan's main problems of the 1990s. They could be asked to imagine that the Japanese government had asked for advice. The task would be to describe the problem, describe three possible solutions, and, for each solution, give its advantages and disadvantages.

The various themes of the Geography curriculum could all stimulate effective homework.

- Tectonic processes could provide 'horror story' types of homework, with pupils required, of course, to make use of particular technical terms. More sympathetic work might be to draft e-mail messages to schools in Kobe, as was done after their earthquake.
- Geomorphological work could produce work of a simple descriptive kind, perhaps writing-up fieldwork on a river course, or of an imaginative kind, such as planning for floods or describing what you would do if caught in a flood. Cross-curricular work, too, such as writing as if a government minister in Bangladesh, could address both geographical and political issues.
- The weather and climate have always been popular topics for homework. The obvious task is to record the weather, and this can be done with increasing complexity over the years. Pupils might be asked

to produce, between them, a booklet of holiday advice, describing the climates of various regions and countries. It is not just that climate affects people, of course, and pupils could be asked for homework to speculate on how human activities affect climate, whether with 'greenhouse gases', deforestation, or 'cloud rustling' (illegal in the USA, under interstate commerce regulations).

- Ecosystems are sensitive to small change. After working on a system, such as a tropical rain forest, groups of pupils could be made 'responsible' for one change (e.g. reducing the number of trees, wiping out a category of animal, polluting a river), with the homework task being to describe how their change might affect the whole system. Reporting back in the following lesson should be a good way of hammocking the work. Interesting work can also be done on the nature of systems themselves, related to Design and Technology, and the complex effects of small changes, related to chaos theory of Maths.

- On population, pupils can, as with many Humanities topics, do engaging survey work, asking peers and adults questions they may not otherwise have considered asking. Interview three people who have not lived in the same place all their lives, one who has moved within this country, and two who have moved between countries. Describe in detail their reasons for moving or migration, as well as their movements. Such a survey could produce a mass of information on the topic, especially if the class has access to a wide variety of travellers. A simpler task would be to ask pupils to write about why they have lived where they have lived, with reasons being given for staying in one place, as much as for moving.

- On settlement, there are many opportunities to do work linked to History topics. Investigation of pupils' neighbourhoods, whether based on local library research, copies of Domesday Book surveys, or following-up the names of roads or buildings, provides opportunities for good group work. Land-use surveys of all kinds can get pupils seeing their own areas with fresh eyes.

- For economic geography work, there are the ever-popular shopping surveys. To give a bit of life to the primary-secondary-tertiary industry divisions, pupils could be asked to interview workers in each type of industry, and back-up the interviews (or substitute for one or more, if there are few local workers in one of the sectors) with research in the school's careers library.

- Development homework tasks could range from the very local, producing plans for local improvements, to the international. A home, school, or supermarket, contain products and materials from all around the world. Pupils could survey such sources, in preparation for work on trade routes or interdependence.

- The environment is popular with pupils, and provides good chances to survey, analyse, plan, campaign, or compare for homework. I've already suggested an environmental journal, in Chapter 7 on Science, and Geography teachers could also work with English, Art, Technology and no doubt other departments on this topic.

Religious Education

There is a continuum of Religious Education syllabuses from the systematic (teaching one religion at a time) to the thematic (teaching one topic at a time, mentioning several religions). Either approach can look at, and will certainly benefit from being based on, important questions and their possible answers. More 'thematic' homework tasks include:

- Research on objects, artefacts and places that are 'special' for pupils, at home or in the neighbourhood.
- Bring in photographs and videos, for example of weddings and other celebrations. Or produce a display of 'seasonal' celebrations, constantly being updated.
- Find out about different symbols, and producing symbols for themselves.
- Describe beliefs that are important to you, and (as another homework) ask other people to describe their beliefs.
- Contemplate. I particularly like the idea of asking pupils to do (almost) nothing for homework: a silence or 'nothingness', however, with great significance.
- On a theme such as 'death', pupils might think about their own lives and write their own obituary (imagining they lived to be 100), and they could ask adults about what they think happens after they die. They might practise writing a letter to a bereaved friend, or do some creative writing having looked at some poetry on the topic.

Homework that forms part of more systematic study of religions can be equally engaging.

- An in-depth investigation of a religion could be done by a whole class, with different pupils, for homework, doing interviews, visits, library research, and imaginative work, on a particular religion.
- Links could be made with other subjects, so homework speculating on the speed of the growth of Islam would benefit from work done in History, and homework on translations of the Bible could be tied in with English. Science and RE surprisingly often cover the same ground: they both ask questions about creation and existence, the purpose or function of different aspects of life, and relationships

between people and 'their' world.

- I've always enjoyed 'story' paintings from the Middle Ages, often on religious themes, and pupils have always enjoyed them too, when I've taken them to galleries. A good homework exercise would be to design a piece of narrative art — perhaps as a whole class — describing key elements of a religion.

CHAPTER 9

Modern Foreign Languages

Modern Foreign Languages (MFL) teachers could be excused for feeling paranoid. Whatever they do, people still say to them 'I spent five years learning French and still can't order a cup of coffee in Paris'. However much the curriculum changes, and ordering coffee becomes a whole term's work, the idea persists that MFL teaching doesn't work. By teaching a subject that is 'tested' in stressful situations (holidays) for the rest of people's lives, MFL teachers are blamed, absurdly, for the consequences of English reserve. Perhaps if Parisian cafés asked tourists to design an experiment to separate a mixture of salt and sand, or demanded an analysis of the religious views of Elizabeth I, MFL teachers might rest easier. However, the fact that MFL are indeed useful and used is also what makes them so important, and in particular makes homework so important. If homework is effective, then MFL teachers have already succeeded in their hardest task: getting pupils to use their new language skills outside the classroom. Next stop, Paris. Some pupils have the advantage of living with the foreign language — most commonly those from French or Spanish speaking countries, but also those learning Welsh as a foreign language but living amongst Welsh speakers. This gives them an advantage, just as it is likely to be advantageous to know already two or three languages, as is the case with most pupils from South Asia, Africa, or Central Europe.

The principles I'd recommend for MFL homework, described here, are related most closely to those for English. Much teaching of Latin, Ancient Greek or Sanskrit follows the same principles as MFL teaching, with attempts made to use modern, if necessarily artificial, sources and contexts: learning how to order a cup of hemlock in an Athenian café, presumably.

- Learning vocabulary is the task most often mentioned by pupils when asked what homework tasks they dislike. Of course, vocabulary needs to be expanded, but there must be ways of doing this that don't put so many pupils off the subject. I have already made suggestions on vocabulary in the chapter on English; here I will add other suggestions. The principle to remember is that vocabulary can be developed in many ways, and that homework tasks should reflect the variety of strategies available.

If pupils want to learn vocabulary without writing or speaking, for example, they could be given written descriptions of people, and asked to draw the people. Or they could match words and pictures, or choose 'friends' from descriptions, or pick out the 10 (or 100) hardest words from a text, or 'draw' words (a 'fat' word, a 'beautiful' word, a 'tall' word, and so on).

Making dictionaries or glossaries, for themselves or for younger pupils, is doubly helpful, just as for History or other subjects. Creating other ways of remembering words, such as making labels for objects around the house or school, can help for a long time after the homework task has been done. A board game — created for homework, of course, with a few simple instructions on the board, and perhaps a set of cards (as in games like Monopoly) could again have long-lasting benefits, and could be used with family members or younger pupils in the school. If the pupils were to choose the best such game, and produce it in large numbers for sale in a school fête, this would be a fine cross-curricular success.

Pupils might write lyrics or even compose songs, to well-known tunes or chants, finding rhymes and rhythms in vocabulary produced by the teacher. I've seen good work on the national anthem and in the style of American army marching chants.

- The MFL curriculum, like the English curriculum, stresses reading, writing, speaking and listening. Homework tasks should involve all of these skills and more, including drawing, music, cooking, mathematical or scientific calculations, and so on. Skills and knowledge from across the whole curriculum can complement, and be complemented by MFL.

Teaching is always a good way of learning, and pupils could be asked to teach a phrase to a member of their family — with the learner recording his or her achievement. Such involvement may seem an obvious technique, but it is done all too little in Secondary schools. Primary schools seem less inhibited.

Pupils might also interview members of their family (in English) about their childhood, as research for work on the perfect tense. With suitable preparation in class, including practising key phrases, pupils could write up these interviews.

Newspapers and magazines are good resources, but pupils may find them off-putting. A useful exercise would be to ask pupils not to read large sections of print, but to use all sorts of clues to 'guess' the topics and content — pictures, names and figures., could all provide useful clues, and pupils could find the techniques useful when it come to reading English papers and magazines, too.

In non-English speaking countries, pupils learn English through films, television and music. However, they don't *always* do this: one of the most frequent comments of school pupils in Sweden was that films and television could be used even more, as they were fashionable and exciting. How can such advantages be replicated in this country? Certainly, no other language has quite the 'pull' of English, but there are 'fashionable' actors, singers, sports stars, and designers, whose words may be similarly underused by many MFL teachers in this country. It is good to see television MFL courses produced by such 'pulls' in recent years. I've not yet seen much use of sports stars, though, and music has moved a long way since teachers could only use tapes of the Eurovision Song Contest. Tape and CD samplers of world music are interesting, including much in French (from Africa and the Caribbean) and Spanish (from Spain and from Latin America). Asking pupils to listen to these — either borrowed to take home, or played at lunchtime or after school — is a good example of apparently easy, but useful, homework.

Nowadays, pupils can get access to materials in different languages on the Internet. A useful homework task would be to search for such materials, or draft contributions to such systems. 'Pen friends' are available, in this way, at the touch of a few buttons, and pupils (like teachers) find such novelty compelling.

Talking is often the final barrier. Pupils reluctant to speak in class may be prepared to do so at home, with a trusted adult or a friend (friends are too often ignored, given the amount of influence they have on homework). If pupils can't even bring themselves to do this, they could still practise in front of a mirror. Some cheap and commonly available computers (most recently-produced ones) can 'voice' text, and it would be a good exercise to get pupils, with access to such computers, to see how they would need to spell words to get the computer to voice them as the French words would sound. My computer, for example, voices 'we' and 'oui' in the same, reasonably accurate, way — for 'yes' in French — but needs 'aufveedersane' for 'goodbye' in German. Presumably there are 'voicing' programmes that 'read' other languages more like native speakers, and there are more expensive CD-Rom programmes that 'talk' in different languages, but using an 'English' voice is probably better for pupils trying to learn the sounds of foreign words, and using a cheaper computer and programs has other obvious advantages. Such exercises are complementary to phonetic transcriptions from tapes, which are slightly lower tech tasks. Phonetic versions of key words were given to British soldiers in France in World War One, with the whole language course on a single postcard.

- Cultural awareness is rightly built in to MFL courses. The skills needed for developing cultural awareness are very closely related to those used in History, Geography, RE, English, and much PSE work. MFL teachers can therefore help and be helped by work on cultural awareness in several subjects.

The European Union is always in the news. The EU is a good source of homework, and even a good source of funding for some projects. MFL teachers could be at the centre of various whole-school projects on the topic. I've heard of mimes, with foreign language 'subtitles'; work on transport, with visits to the Channel Tunnel (and if possible France or Belgium, through it); international competitions and surveys, using visits, letters or computer links; and industrial work, with pan-European companies keen to involve or at least inform pupils. All such work is ideal for homework or for special 'cross-curricular' days.

A simple bit of history could be built on. The croissant, a favourite bit of French baking, was apparently invented as an insult to the Turkish flag, after bakers had helped relieve the siege of Budapest in 1686. What other aspects of French life have such vivid histories? Pupils could be asked to research, or to speculate. Cartoons, often highlighting stereotypes and so needing to be used sensitively, are good sources of information about countries and cultures at different times in History.

Food preferences are interesting. I was told by an Italian teacher that the best item of English food, relished whenever she came here, was milk. Pupils could survey people from different countries (depending on their access to such people), or could infer tastes from newspapers and magazines. Supermarkets are good sources, these days, of 'potted' culture (as well as croissants). Pupils could be asked to find and report back on foods and other goods from, or popular in, the country or culture being studied. There might even be prizes for discovering unusual foods.

- Trips abroad organised by MFL staff are still popular, especially in the South of England, and may well become even more popular as the rail network speeds up. These trips should be able to count as homework. It may be appropriate to add up the time pupils spend speaking or listening to French, which may be only an hour or two on a day trip, and call that their homework for a couple of weeks. Certainly, preparation for, and follow-up to, trips makes for ideal homework tasks. Altogether, a day trip may well take care of a month's homework tasks.

MFL teachers can set up 'mock' trips abroad, with classes running a 'French' café for other pupils or parents, planning for this as homework. A whole school day may be turned over to another language, or a set of languages or cultures. 'Multicultural' fairs have become popular, especially in places with varied populations. Of course, there is more to a country than can be 'made up' in this way, but preparing for such events provides many good learning opportunities, even if the final result is not entirely authentic.

Instead of learning another language on a trip, pupils could gain insights into language learning by working on how people learn English. Producing a guide to the UK or English for foreign visitors, taking into account the language and culture of the visitors, would help pupils when they do the reverse.

CILT have produced a whole book of homework ideas in MFL. If only other subject associations and support groups were as efficient at supporting homework.

CHAPTER 10

Art, Music and Design and Technology

In the early days of the Technical and Vocational Education Initiative, I asked an advisor what 'technology' meant, as TVEI seemed to range so wide. I was told that technology marked the border between 'learning about' and 'doing' or 'applying', so that learning about economic theory wasn't technology, running a mini-company was; learning the words for ordering a meal in French wasn't, going to France and ordering a meal was; reading about archaeological finds wasn't, digging for finds was. This wonderfully broad definition of technology encompasses most effective learning, and certainly encompasses nearly all Art, Music, Design and Technology, Drama, Physical Education, IT, Business Studies, Work Experience, School Councils, most visits out of school and much project work in every subject. To separate out Art, Music and Design and Technology, as I have done for this chapter, because of the 'technology' link between them — all involving learning about, planning, creating, and evaluating tangible products — is therefore a little narrow. Nevertheless, it seems that, when it comes to homework, the challenges and opportunities of these three subject areas have much in common, and these common factors are not always shared with other more or less 'technological' subjects.

- All three subjects (all five, or more, if you split Design and Technology into some of its constituent parts) enable every pupil to produce something — a picture, a song, a cake — that has its own existence, its own originality. These products are what families expect from the subjects, and families enjoy getting a 'thing' in answer to the question 'what did you make in school today?' So the products, when they are made, can affirm the school's work, and the learning of the pupil, in a way that an essay or a set of calculations rarely can. Homework should make use of this enthusiasm.
- The act of production is also the activity that best motivates pupils: they may spend hours working on a picture, playing an instrument,

constructing a model, even if it has nothing to do with school. Such practical work is therefore ideal for homework, yet the obvious problem is that most homes are not equipped for much practical work. Several schools overcome this problem by getting pupils to do 'homework' in school: lunchtime choirs or bands, after-school art clubs, producing food for a Parents Evening. This seems a good way of approaching homework, and a good use of school resources, as long as staffing such clubs is not taken for granted!

- Homes may not always be equipped for practical work, but all homes are packed with the products of artists, musicians and designers. Many of these products, however, are unrecognised, ironically, because they are 'popular'. I used to find it strange to hear of a house described as 'architect-designed', as though other houses just came together by chance, until I realised that the phrase 'architect-designed' referred to the status, pay, and qualifications of the person designing the house, not the fact that it was 'more' designed than other houses. Homework can help pupils to become more aware of the 'designedness' of their environments.

- For many years, people have tended to think of artists, musicians and designers as individual creative spirits, and products as easily attributable to such single geniuses. This belies the cooperative creativity of past times and other cultures, such as the emergence and development of folk songs, vernacular architecture, or decorative sculptures on Medieval cathedrals. It also belies the cooperative nature of much of what is thought of as 'solo' creativity, with debates over the contributions of uncredited painters in ceramic workshops of 'names' like Clarice Cliff, or the influence of producers and session musicians on 'stars' like Lennon and McCartney. The cooperative creativity demonstrated here is not a problem, unless you are the person being accused of being 'less of a genius', but an opportunity, a potential strength, and it can play a big role in the way in which Art, Music and Design and Technology are taught, and how homework can be set.

- Evaluation is a key skill in all these subjects, and is terribly hard to teach. One way of generating views on a product is to get pupils to ask other people what they think. In such a way, pupils can summarise and perhaps adjudicate between the evaluations of other people, rather than always coming up with an original evaluation of their own.

The examples of homework tasks, below, are divided into the three subjects, though I would hate to discourage cross-curricular work.

Art

Art is significant for developing pupils' self image, and investigating stereotypes, just as much as it is a way of developing technical skills and aesthetic values. Pupils learn to look at themselves and other around them, to observe their home and school, and the environment beyond. Art can be a way into cultures that are otherwise impenetrable, and a way of linking otherwise diverse traditions and cultures. In all of these ways, Art can be justified as an ideal focus for imaginative homework. The engagement that is a theme running through so much of this book is easily envisaged by teachers and pupils of the subject. A simple task such as sketching a member of your household, or doing a close observation study of your own front door, can help a pupil understand both the object of the study and the methods of capturing it. As pupils produce artefacts themselves, and come to a greater knowledge and understanding of the art and artefacts of artists and craftspeople past and present, they can develop raise their own self-esteem an raise the esteem in which they hold others. Such cross-curricular skills are complemented by links with other subjects, whether looking at propaganda posters (linking with History), maps and the local and world environment (Geography), plants, and natural and made patterns (Science), repeated patterns (isometric and tessellated patterns) (Maths), or 3D modelling (Design and Technology). Such links with other areas of the curriculum are worth pointing out, not because Art needs such links to justify itself, but because other teachers, like pupils and their families, might better understand the value of Art to them.

- Engagement with people is a theme of many of my homework suggestions, and appears again in Art. Self-portraits, and portraits of friends and family, have been central to European Art for centuries. Pupils can follow in that tradition, and doing the work (or doing preparatory sketches) at home, away from peer pressure, can give opportunities for more personal insights.
  Art teachers are well practised at working with pupils on more complex forms of portraiture, as well as 'representative' self-portraits, and these, too, can make good homework tasks. Shields and boxes may be researched or made at home, where pupils can safely think about what characteristics or possessions or associations best describe them. It would make sense for one stage of this work to involve asking family members to say what they think are the most important characteristics of the pupil. Working on objects that pupils feel are important, and on characteristics they value or are proud of, is a vital aspect of PSE work, too. In Chapter 11, I've suggested PSE work on dreams, and these too

could be used as the basis of interesting 'psychological' portraiture. There are many possible uses of photographs. Either the original copies, or, preferably, duplicates, of photographs of the pupil could be put together into a composite portrait, in the style of David Hockney's work. Hockney was concerned, in his photographic work, to show many views of the same person or scene. It is such multi-perspective work that made his choice of photography so interesting, but before him, Cubists had done similar work, as had religious painters throughout the Middle Ages, with later portraits, such as those done of the Elizabethans, often being more subtle collections of perspectives, with meaningful views out of windows and significant objects left 'casually' on tables in the background.

Homework looking at, sketching, and picturing other people, in the forms suggested for self-portraits is also engaging. Pupils may never have really looked at people in their families, and if Art homework does nothing else, it will have achieved a lot if it gets pupils to do this.

- Engagement with homes and neighbourhoods is a way of making homework necessary, that is, impossible to be done in class.

Group work on 'our homes', and later on 'our school', with each pupil contributing to a large display, can be done in many ways. The simplest technique would involve sketching at home, with final versions produced in class, but more complex work might, for example, mean colour matching decor and furniture (using colour charts or colours from magazine photographs), followed by attempts to mix the same colours in class, or pupils could be asked to sketch different parts of their homes (one sketching a kitchen ceiling, one a front door) to produce a composite picture of a class 'home'.

Out into the garden or down the road, for good cross-curricular work on the environment (Geography, Science and a cross-curricular theme), street furniture (Technology), architecture (Technology and History), and so on. Pupils could produce guide books for visitors to their areas (English, Geography), or campaign leaflets to protect the beauty of the area or to highlight problems of pollution (Geography). They could plan trips to parks and rivers, including the 'artistic opportunities', for younger pupils or for their own class. They could research detailed themes, such as bricks or leaves or gates or shop signs. And they could all do such work in and around the school as well as in their homes.

- Art includes work on the functional as well as aesthetic value of artefacts, and the work, above, on the environment, could be extended to involve the design of new street furniture or shop signs, or environmental improvements.

Other design work, based on investigations done for homework, could include posters for events or services, illustrations for magazines or brochures, signs for use around the school during Parents' Evenings, or icons for use in guides — as the Olympics have sporting icons for each discipline.

- Investigations are as important to Art as they are to Geography or Science or Maths. By investigative work, here, I mean in-depth research, where the value lies in the process of the research as much as in any product based on it.

Gallery and museum trips may be organised in school time, but if pupils can be persuaded to search out exhibitions for homework, there are opportunities for a greater variety of work, and a more individual experience for each pupil. Such a task could be set as a holiday homework, or as a long-term homework, to allow flexibility and the greatest possible variety. A regular spot in class, where pupils report to the rest of the class on an exhibition they've seen, could hammock such work. Virtual trips can also be arranged. Some 'galleries' are now available on CD-Roms, and pupils could also research from exhibition catalogues. A simple task, for any exhibition visit, is to choose the three pictures or objects you would take to a desert island. I was impressed, on one occasion, when a pupil made a rather unusual choice, of a painting that few other pupils found at all interesting, but was less impressed when he justified his choice: it had the largest quantity of wood in the frame, so he could build a raft and escape the island.

Although finding Old Masters that can be investigated for homework may be a bit of a challenge, especially for younger pupils, houses are full of other art and craft products to be studied, including textiles, ceramics, and graphics. Similarly, pupils could be set the task of 'finding' colours (for collage work) or objects with particular textures or shapes (for collage work or mosaics).

My favourite Art and English book, *Double Vision* by Michael and Peter Benton, includes pictures (such as Bruegel's 'Children's Games') with poems written about them (by William Carlos Williams, in this instance), and poems (such as Tennyson's 'Lady of Shalott') with pictures inspired by them (by Holman Hunt, in this instance). What a good way of investigating art (and poetry), whether the investigation uses the Bentons' book, or simply asks pupils to do similar work, based on their own choice of paintings.

- Awe and wonder can accompany artistic activities, as they can accompany work in Religious Education or Science. It is interesting to try to create homework tasks that could produce such responses.

Simply looking at the sky at night (as also recommended as a Science homework) can have the desired effect, and so may a study done from a great height — perhaps from an aircraft journey during a holiday, or from the top of a high building or mountain. Close observation of objects under a microscope could be similarly stunning, and might be done outside lessons, perhaps in after-school Science clubs.

I've seen pupils look at newborn or very young babies with the same sense of awe, and although such studies may be difficult to set for homework, a visit from a teacher on maternity leave, or from a parent or sibling of a pupil with a young baby, could allow for study to be done outside lessons, at least. Doing the work in a lesson might be difficult and might upset the baby, especially with a large class, and this is why I'd recommend it for homework.

Music

I've heard Music teachers say that they are unable to set Music homework. I find that a puzzling view, especially as instrumental tuition, often organised by school Music departments, depends on homework to a greater extent than just about any other subject. Still, even those teachers who say they can't set Music homework, often do get pupils to do Music outside lessons: choirs, bands, orchestras, working hard every week and maybe performing in shows and competitions. As a general rule, where pupils are active in such groups, this should be counted as, or towards, homework. Non-active pupils may be asked to do alternative homework, if the system is to be seen to be scrupulously fair. Perhaps it would be best to set some traditional homework for all pupils, with non-active pupils expected to do more, or to be monitored more carefully.

National Curriculum Music stresses both performance and theory — though it was a fight to keep the high profile for performance. Most performance homework will, I guess, be done in school music groups, as I've said, outside lessons but not actually at home. Nevertheless, Music homework done at home needn't be wholly passive. I would hate to encourage the sort of passive Music work described by Billy Connolly, in whose 'music appreciation' lessons, the pupils were played music whilst being ordered to 'Appreciate! Appreciate!'.

● The first group of homework tasks are investigative ones, based on the principle that in Music, as in Art, the object of the study is readily, almost universally, available, but too often ignored or taken for granted.

Although radio stations have big audiences amongst pupils, there is a greater variety of styles of music on television programmes, as the music may be central to the programme but is more often used in title sequences, in the background to 'create atmosphere', or in adverts. It is the television that introduces most pupils to classical music, even if classical composers and performers might feel their works are served badly by being chopped up into tiny pieces to accompany sports programmes or cat food advertisements. Pupils continue listening to more classical music on the television than they do in music lessons, and investigating the television classical repertoire must be a valuable homework exercise. Pupils may be asked to describe styles, or research for a class quiz (spot the advertisement?), or describe instrumentation on particular pieces, or try to find out who the composers are.

Pupils could do a critical review of television music, and as an extension of this, could act as producers themselves, and either choose a product and find music (from a selection offered by the teacher) to suit it, or be given a piece of music, and write about what sort of product it could be used for. The three main uses of music on television (outside music shows), for advertisements, titles, and backgrounds, could be investigated and 'produced' as separate activities. It is worth noting that some music composed for film and television has a significant status in its own right: not just the work of William Walton, but that of people like the largely unknown Scott Bradley, composer of many of the best Tom and Jerry soundtracks. Tom and Jerry's interpretation of Liszt (in *Cat Concerto*), is rather more respectful than that of Ken Russell (in *Lisztomania*), too.

'Pop' music, in recent years, seems to have drawn on almost every musical style, way beyond its folk and blues roots, with influences from the Americas, Africa, South Asia, and many parts of Europe. There must be valuable investigative work here, and pupils who can spot the influences of Bangra, or Native American songs, or Flamenco, or West African High Life, should be better prepared for the comparatively straightforward 'spotting' exercises in GCSE exams.

Investigating any form of music, wherever it is heard, can help pupils listen more critically. An exercise involving matching sets of words to pieces of music can be useful in many ways, and can be set as a very regular homework. The title or other information about the music could be at the top of the page, with qualities such as tempo, pitch, dynamics, or texture down the left-hand side, and qualifiers such as slow, moderate, fast (for tempo) across the page. Pupils could fill in such sheets whilst listening to the music, and the results of such surveys, including ways of improving the descriptive words, could be the basis of much class work.

A form of engagement, similar to work in several other subjects, is a music survey. Pupils could create surveys, in class, of likes and dislikes and of more complex issues like favoured music in particular situations (journeys, homework, shops, ice rinks and so on.). Their homework would be to carry out the surveys, with family members and friends. The age and sex of the respondents might be included, to make for a more subtle analysis.

Assemblies may rarely be the focus for communal singing, as they were in the past, but many encourage music, either performed by small groups of pupils (related to a particular theme or as part of an 'achievements' assembly), or using records. Where possible, music homework could involve preparation or research for such events.

- Scoring music is found difficult by many pupils, in the way that some pupils have difficulty writing in a foreign language, and some, indeed, have difficulty writing in English. It is precisely the difficulty of the topic that made me want to think of homework tasks, because if homework can be set on this, it can be set on any area of Music.

In English and MFL teaching books, pupils are sometimes encouraged to transcribe phonetically, without worrying about accurate spelling at first, so that anxiety is reduced, and so that pupils involve themselves more in the sounds heard. The same could be said for music, with a homework task being to pick a piece of music, in any form, and 'draw' the music. Various possible symbols, and methods of denoting qualities of the music, could be discussed in the prior lessons, and pupils, after doing the homework, might be asked to explain and justify their notation, or other pupils could try to guess the music so described. Another technique used by History and English teachers is called 'sequencing', where pupils are given small sections of writing and are asked to put them in order: sometimes there is a single correct order, sometimes there are many viable orders. For Music, pupils could be given various staff-notated phrases, and asked to order them, and justify their ordering.

- Songs have a special place in the Music curriculum, even though singing seems to have a much smaller role in schools than it did in previous years. As songs have words, there are 'easy' connections with other curriculum areas, most obviously English. Songs are also the most popular music form for pupils, and happily have become more and more eclectic.

Music teachers must have had mixed feelings when a British teen band recently had a hit with a cover version of an American song based on a Chopin Prelude. Was this worth pointing out to pupils? A good use that might be made of such a connection, would be to see if pupils might plunder more of the instrumental repertoire, in any style, and make a song. Alternatively, they might match or adapt ready-made lyrics and tunes, to suit certain styles: the National Curriculum mentions lullabies and sea shanties.

Many songs, in different traditions, contain a very simple motif or 'hook' (in pop music). These can be remarkably simple — a single note repeated in a simple rhythm, two or three notes at the most, often with a matching simplicity of words. After classwork trying to isolate such elements of songs, pupils could be asked to compose hooks of their own. I've seen work on doh ray and me, with pupils asked to compose tunes made up only of these notes. Composing hooks might be made easier for pupils if they were given such a limited choice, and the words, too, might be restricted.

Songs are used for political purposes — good illustrations of this are in films like *Oh What a Lovely War*, or *Cabaret*, or the songs sung at political party conferences. When studying national identities in History, pupils might study nationalist songs in Music, including Jacobite songs from Scotland and anthems from other parts of the UK and beyond. War songs could be studied, along with anti-war songs. Homework tasks might be to make comparisons between such songs, or compose their own examples. Subverting songs for a different purpose has a long tradition, and such subversion, too, might make a good homework task.

- Finally, I would reiterate the need to acknowledge performance outside classes as valid homework tasks. I would add to the list of school performances all instrumental lessons, and the practice to back them up, religious singing, and maybe even a few football songs (if pupils can be persuaded to analyse them).

Design and Technology

Design and Technology has established its place in the curriculum, but not without a few uncertainties and confusions. For me, the subject 'arrived' when a parent of a 10-year old told me excitedly about her son's work on rat traps, after a History topic on the Plague. The most exciting thing, for him, in an exciting project, had been comparing the designs and final products of the different pupils, and working out how their own products could be improved. It was the first time I'd heard the investigative and evaluative aspects of the subject promoted as its main strength and attraction. When it comes to homework, investigation and design are clearly easier to set up than manufacturing, but the making, if mostly done in class, can hammock other kinds of homework. Pupils may be impatient to get on with making things, and find it difficult to be enthusiastic about the early stages of design, or later evaluations. These pupils could reasonably be set such disliked tasks for homework, having to complete them before being allowed to make things in class. Better still to set such interesting homework tasks that pupils are converted to the joys of the whole of Design and Technology.

- Investigative work is ideal for Design and Technology homework, and has much in common with many other subjects.

Chairs can be investigated well for homework, with the range of their uses in homes and school, and their symbolic uses, such as thrones or 'chairs' of meetings, can stimulate book research, too.

Items from around the house have always been popular with Design and Technology teachers, whether looking at kettles, window locks, mugs, or items of clothing or jewellery. Pupils can study them to get ideas for class work, or to look for more subtle distinctions such as the difference between incrementally and radically changed styles.

It may be possible to study more complex equipment, working on systems that play music or flush toilets or change gears on bicycles. Sketches and other descriptions, or even occasionally the equipment itself, may be brought in to class for further, collective, study.

Tension and compression in bridges is popular with engineering courses, and can make good holiday tasks: any pupil can find a bridge, even if they don't travel away on holiday, and the whole class's collection of sketches should make for impressive display work. Perhaps there could be a prize for the greatest variety of bridges seen by one pupil, or the most unusual design seen or most accurately 'annotated' sketch.

People, too, easily available outside class, can be investigated, with work investigating the use of, and consumer-testing, toys for children, or cutlery for adults. Such work is an integral part of 'real' industry, and the more systematic the surveying, the better.

You could also ask pupils to keep a food diary for a period of time, followed up with work in class on food types and 'balanced' diets. Food consumption by others could also be surveyed, although, as for individual pupils, sensitivity will be needed to avoid exacerbating food problems. Preference surveys can be less intrusive, and can be done in the same form as those for products.

It may be a stereotype of children being able to help explain electronic equipment to adults, but a homework task asking them to do this, based on finding out exactly what the difficulties are, and perhaps writing up their advice in an instruction booklet, could be an interesting longer term or holiday task. 'Help' tasks, as well as being interesting in design terms, are helpful in encouraging pupils to take responsibility. I've seen tasks involving designing for disabled people, which can be valuable; I've also found that pupils are interested to know, for example, that a famous 'range' cooker was designed by a man who was blind. Turning the exercise around, so that pupils think about how disabled people might themselves design, should increase their imaginative skills.

- Designing tasks can be completed as homework, whether designing products or diets, and, although drawing boards and good quality paper may not be appropriately taken home, preparatory sketching and early drafts of final designs certainly can be done outside the classroom.

Design can be and often is a collective activity for professional designers, yet collective design doesn't seem to be very common in school. Pupils could be asked to work as groups, for homework, and this is enjoyed by many pupils who therefore have an excuse to get together at lunchtime or after school. Otherwise, pupils can be asked to work on different aspects of a design problem, with the results being put together in class. Designing a bedsit, including its furnishings, for example, includes many separate tasks for individuals or small groups of pupils.

Some pupils may be attracted to slightly surreal design tasks. There's a poem by Yeats, saying 'I made my song a coat'. Why not? Perhaps pupils could design a 'song coat' or other bizarre objects. Expensive gift shops have, in recent years, stocked a few surreal products, for further inspiration.

Following earlier survey work, pupils could of course be asked to design new products, such as sports-based games for children, or easy-to-use remote control devices for adults.

Socially useful designs, such as waste removal machines, equipment for getting cats out of trees, or bicycles or more general road safety equipment, are good subjects for homework, as pupils should feel more committed to such 'important' design.

- Making is so important — Design and Technology teachers tell the delightful and I hope true story that 'wrighting' was one of the original Three Rs, until an MP misspelt it 'writing'. (Teachers of moral education or social reformers presumably lay claim to 'righting' as a convincing member of the Three Rs.) Making things at home is popular with Primary schools, and can be carried into Secondary schools, although the limitations and inequalities, related to equipment and materials, require careful planning.

One style of making done at home, and well practised in Primary school, is to use 'improvised' materials, or rubbish, such as boxes, straws, or packaging, to make products that can be brought into school. Older pupils should be slightly more responsible 'recyclers' than Primary children.

Cooking is done in every home, so carefully arranged homework tasks involving cooking should be possible, whatever equipment and materials are available. Flexibility is needed, so pupils can match their work to their circumstances.

CHAPTER 11

Physical Education and Personal and Social Education

Considering the position of Physical Education (PE) and Personal and Social Education (PSE), alongside English, as the most home-taught subjects, it is surprising that most schools set little or no homework. Pupils will have developed sophisticated physical and social skills well before they see a school, and school-age pupils carry on developing physically and socially, outside school, whether or not these developments always match PE and PSE syllabuses. A large part of this chapter will be an attempt to help teachers and pupils to acknowledge the non-school learning that does go on, so that it can be deemed homework, rather than simply adding a list of new, extra, homework tasks.

The life-and-death relevance of PE and PSE contrast with the low status they often have in schools, amongst pupils and staff alike. Many who dislike PE are prepared to say that it should be voluntary: few would dare say the same about the similarly disliked Maths. The status of PSE is harmed in a different way, by the practice in many schools of letting or making any teacher teach it, whether or not they have any specialist training, skills, or interest. Both subjects have reduced status as a result of the lack of exams and qualifications, with a small proportion of pupils going on to GCSE PE, and even fewer gaining distinct qualifications in 'Life Skills' or other PSE-based qualifications. Other countries give the subjects more or less weight. The USA, for example, makes PE a high status subject, with a more middle-class image than it has in the UK. France, in contrast, leaves much PSE work to non-teaching staff. In schools where PE and PSE do have a low status, this can be used to the advantage of teachers: they can use teaching strategies, and set homework tasks, that are much more imaginative and varied than they would 'get away with' in other, more vigilantly monitored, subjects.

Physical Education

Young people may be less fit than they were. This probably has little to do with the amount of time spent on school sports, but much more to do with life outside lessons. Homework, or physical activities outside school, are therefore enormously important aspects of PE. Walking to school, or sitting with good posture, or playing active games, or carrying shopping, or decorating your bedroom, or washing the car, can all be, and count as, PE homework, if they help pupils improve their skills, strength and endurance.

- A regular 'exercise audit' can be set as homework, listing and recording physical activities done. As with 'homework audits', pupils who are dishonest may become more open if they are told how ineffective their apparent hard work is, given their current level of achievement in school.
- Games are part of PE and part of pupils' lives outside school. Surveying and describing games, including the games of younger sisters and brothers, or games played in a local park, can help pupils understand their variety. There are many variations on more standard games, and describing the 'alternative rules' of such games can be a challenging task. For longer projects, the history of particular games could be investigated.
- Homework can be done on creating games or activities with sets of rules invented by the pupils. Trying to invent a game with three of the advantages of football and three of the advantages of rugby, having worked on those advantages in class, might lead to interesting hybrid games. It is worth pointing out to pupils, that most of the world's most popular games have been formally described or 'invented' very recently, and several have come out of schools.
- Outdoor activities, developing leadership and cooperative skills, may not be so common these days, outside school. However, I've seen imaginative work on 'mock' expeditions, such as the family's expedition to the supermarket, including descriptions of dangers, solutions to difficult problems (such as parking the car next to a pillar), or fitness challenges (such as getting the ice cream home before it melts).
- Pupils may get exercise outside school. I've heard pupils, in the build-up to exams, recommend exercise, as a way of solving the boredom and stress of revision. Revision can be done whilst on an exercise bike, and memory games can be played while running or swimming. As homework, this would have the magical property of combining two homework tasks in the time it takes to do either one of them.
- Another doubly efficient game that could be encouraged for homework

is round-the-house chess, invented by computer pioneers Alan Turing and David Champernowne. Make your move in a chess match, run around the house (or to the end of the street and back, or to the ground floor and back), and if you get back before your opponent has moved, you get another go. The game could be adapted to use any other board game, and to computer games too. Older pupils might adapt it as a revision exercise, setting each other tasks: 'name 10 parts of a cell', 'write down six important causes of World War One'.

- A difficult out-of-class activity, sometimes set as GCSE coursework, asks pupils to arrange tournaments. If pupils can do this, it would certainly be a good homework task. Analysing the organisational skills used by other tournament managers could be easier to achieve. If life is a game, then pupils could reasonably be asked to organise a 'healthy life' plan for themselves, too.

- Understanding the need for fair play, and appropriate responses to success and failure, is an important personal skill. I've seen pupils exhibit such understanding while looking after younger children so a good homework task would be to supervise children at play, perhaps in school (or in a local Primary school) at lunchtime, with reports being written about how the younger children are or fail to be 'fair'.

- Watching television sport may be the cause of physical problems rather than a source of solutions, but homework tasks could make slightly better use of this time, encouraging pupils to write reviews of matches or competitions.

Personal and Social Education

Personal and Social Education lessons may be taught by tutors and be largely administrative periods; they may be linked to or incorporate RE; they may be covered by specialists and include substantial amounts of sex education and/or careers work. PSE is generally the only separate lesson in school that is not named as a separate subject in the National Curriculum. 'Traditional' homework often seems inappropriate (and unwelcome), as it's not a 'traditional' learn and examine subject. But unconventional homework — tasks in fact that might not be called homework — are suited to PSE. The suggestions below apply to some of the common topics taught in PSE, but syllabuses may incorporate topics that I've written about in other sections, including PE, above.

- Study skills are often taught or promoted in PSE, although it can be a little dangerous to separate study skills from the subjects being studied. A simple homework would be to list the time spent on homework (as in Chapter 30), produce revision plans, or list resources needed or got (like distractions and aids to learning listed in Chapter 2).

- Self-assessment homework (as described in Chapter 5) can also get pupils thinking about their studies outside the influence of peers, and with concerned members of their families. I find it helpful to get parents or carers to countersign such self-assessments.

- Where careers is taught within PSE, homework could include searching out appropriate (or even inappropriate) jobs from advertisements in local papers, to be brought in to school for applications to be drafted. Alternatively, the applications could be drafted for homework. More unusual homework tasks would be to prepare for mock interviews in class, with pupils preparing questions to ask other candidates as well as answers they may give themselves. Research could also be done on one job or place of work, with a class building up a collection of materials to be kept in the careers library.

- There's a family 'survival guide', written by Robin Skynner and John Cleese, and this could be the basis of subtle PSE work including homework — as families are 'survived' at home. Teachers might get pupils to write their own specialist guides for homework: I've seen good work on how to survive weddings or Christmas. Survival in school could also be studied enthusiastically by pupils outside your lesson. 'How to make your teacher feel wanted' is an exercise, invented by psychology students who arranged, before a lecture, to look enthusiastic on one side of the room (leaning forward, making eye-contact with the lecturer) and uninterested on the other side of the room: the lecturer gradually moved towards the 'interested' side, and addressed every remark to that side. By practising such techniques, pupils can come to realise that they can affect teachers (in positive ways) just as the teachers can affect them.

- Work on bullying is always welcome, and pupils might do surveys for homework. Specialist materials are now easily available. (My previous book, *Learning to Teach*, has a section on it.) As part of the work on bullying, or as a separate topic, pupils could be given training in assertiveness. Homework related to this could be simply to practice some of the techniques, that is, to say no, or to repeat a request clearly and without anger (the 'broken record' technique), or to 'fog' unwelcome remarks (as in 'well I may be fat but at least I've got better manners than you'). Pupils enjoy practising such techniques on each other, as a game, and will I hope use them 'for real', too.

- Finally, ask your pupils to fall asleep for homework. Surely none can object to this. In the next PSE lesson, work on dream analysis. I like the book *Dream Power* by Ann Faraday, to guide such work, but I've not seen copies of it for several years. Teachers could use any of a number of more or less convincing guides to dreams, and a surprising amount of good PSE work can be created out of the pupils' dreams. A rule must be, of course, that the pupils choose which dreams to report to the class, and which to keep to themselves.

CHAPTER 12

Cross-curricular issues and Information Technology

Cross-curricular issues have had such a peculiar status in English and Welsh schools since 1988, that I feel obliged to give a bit of an historical introduction. Until 1988, the only legally compulsory subject was RE, and the content of this was not specified. Issues deemed 'cross-curricular' since 1988 only became so after the curriculum was defined in terms of subjects, so that all the topics that didn't fit neatly into those 11 'named' subjects became 'cross' (as we all were at the time). As English was 'named' in 1988, it lost its cross-curricular status ('English across the curriculum'), replaced by its cousin, 'communication', a cross-curricular skill. As Sociology and Social Studies were not named in the 1988 Act, they became submerged in cross-curricular dimensions, skills and themes. Information Technology did a little dance all of its own: a cross-curricular skill *and* a part of Technology, from 1988, it later outgrew Technology to become a named subject on its own, whilst remaining, really, an enhanced cross-curricular skill. Sex education hovers between Science and the cross-curricular skill of PSE. Environmental issues are specified in Geography and Science, but also appear as a cross-curricular theme. Latin, Greek, Child Care, Motor Vehicle Studies, Media Studies, and several other subjects lost out completely: those schools that retain them may justify them in terms of cross-curricular issues, but more usually just fit them in around the National Curriculum.

So the 1988 Act determined a 'broad and balanced curriculum', covering 12 secondary subjects (13 in Wales) and promoting 'the spiritual, moral, cultural, mental and physical development of pupils at school and in society' and preparing pupils 'for the opportunities, responsibilities and experiences of adult life'. The National Curriculum Council had to come up with definitions of the cross-curricular issues. There were to be cross-curricular dimensions, skills and themes. Cross-curricular dimensions, seeping into all subjects, provided equal opportunities and education for life in a multicultural society. Cross-curricular skills, shared between subjects, covered communication, numeracy, study skills, problem solving, personal and social education, and IT. Cross-curricular themes covered economic and industrial understanding, and careers, health, citizenship and environmental education. The Welsh, in a parallel universe, came up with aspects of learning, themes, competences, and dimensions. The (English or Welsh) cross-curricular guidance could be interpreted quite flexibly, unlike the subject guidance, and the OFSTED inspection system, set up a few years later, seemed to focus on the 11 subjects more than on the cross-curricular issues. Schools have therefore treated them in many different ways, so my guidance, too, needs to reflect this complexity and variety. I have kept PSE in another chapter, as it is so often timetabled as a separate subject. On the other hand, I've kept IT in this chapter, even though, with the revision of the Technology curriculum, it has been given a separate 'subject' existence all of its own. IT stays here, as it is often taught within other subjects, and it has, in any case, a lot in common with the other cross-curricular issues.

There are two approaches to teaching cross-curricular issues, suggested in this chapter. One is to cover issues entirely within other subjects, with the school simply needing to do an audit of what is taught, where, and how. This is the most common approach to 'communication', for example, where schools may develop sophisticated language and communication policies, but these will apply across the board. The second approach is the 'extra-curricular' approach, where issues are covered outside traditional lessons, perhaps on a regular basis every few weeks, perhaps as an end-of-year 'special' time. This approach may include work that would not normally be thought of as teaching at all, such as establishing a School Council, but which does nonetheless promote many skills.

- Cross-curricular issues developed within subjects.
  To develop skills or personal organisation and study skills, along with a positive attitude to school, I would recommend that the first few weeks of Year 7 should have carefully planned and coordinated homework tasks. It would be a good idea to give pupils a single booklet containing homework in every subject for two or three weeks, including which nights each homework should be done, and when they should be handed in. A booklet like this would of course need to be planned and agreed by all staff, but it shouldn't take long, as teachers would not be asked to set more work, just to plan it in advance. A theme like 'Myself' or 'Home and School' could link homework in every subject, and such topic work would be familiar to most pupils from their Primary schools. On 'Myself', English homework might include a language history, Maths might involve work on

measurements, Science might do a homework on pulses, History on a personal time-line. Geography homework could be on places visited, RE on a personal symbol, MFL on saying 'my name is ...' in different languages. Art could include a self-portrait, Music a survey of musical tastes, and Technology a study of favourite objects or food. PE could set a homework of a health and fitness audit, and IT might require pupils to put all the information collected into a form that could be entered in to a database.

Work on 'citizenship' is done in many subjects, and it is useful for homework to focus on links between these approaches. I've recommended in earlier chapters joint History and Music work on nationalism, and pupils could similarly do joint English and Maths work on elections, or MFL and Geography work on the influence of Napoleon's reforms on modern France. A standard homework task on citizenship, and on the other themes, skills and dimensions, could be to write a report that makes use of knowledge and skills gained in each subject. It is the sort of task usually left to teachers, when writing a policy document on the ways in which the school meets the cross-curricular issues, so it should be a welcome relief to get pupils to do this work.

Several subjects might cover an event, and skills and themes can be developed, especially if the subject teachers coordinate such work. There are too many pupils who, just before Christmas, make the same cards in several lessons, as a card is, of course, relevant to Art, Design and Technology, RE, PSE, and (with 'Joyeux Noel') MFL. Homework on such an event, whether Christmas, the Olympics, or a volcanic eruption, with varied tasks set by different teachers, should enhance the 'balance' of the curriculum, and allow pupils to feel that they are cheating a little, as information and skills from one subject can be used for another. As pupils move into the upper years, the importance of careers is increasingly recognised, although too few subjects formally build it in to the curriculum (MFL being a noble exception). Those pupils doing vocational courses, or studying GCSEs within a vocational framework, are likely to get the best deal, but all pupils deserve 'relevant' studies, with the significance of paid work recognised and appropriate skills developed. Homework tasks such as comparing work in the early 20th century and today (in History), or interpreting pay slips (in Maths), should be helpful.

Critical analysis of subjects can be done for homework. A simple task would be to count up (for Maths?) the number of men and women appearing in texts or on displays used in each subject, with a prize (in a confident school) for the least imbalanced department. I've seen good work on ethnicity and displays around the school, and this could be led by the Art department, perhaps. Pupils could also analyse subjects for their contributions to the environment (perhaps run by the Geography department), or to an understanding of Europe or of the World.

- Cross-curricular issues developed outside subject lessons.

Whole-school projects might include making a video about the school and its pupils, perhaps for use as a marketing device, or making improvements around the school, painting murals, organising the library, and improving classroom displays. These can be done as regular homework tasks, or as out-of-class activities on special days. Theme parks now have education departments, stressing the many cross-curricular and subject issues covered by a visit. Any trip out of school could do much the same, if teachers are willing to produce enough imaginative materials. Homework of the form 'go out and have fun' should be welcome, even if the sentence ends 'oh, and fill in these worksheets when you get back'.

A School Council, as I've already said, is educative and usually done as homework, outside lessons. I've tried to get older pupils to make a choice between joining such a Council, supporting younger pupils with their homework, coaching sports teams, or taking part in a community group. Given the choice, pupils can at least feel as though the activity is really theirs, and such 'prefect' work has a whole range of benefits for the pupils and for the school as a whole.

Many schools will welcome prospective pupils, in the year or two before they come to the school. Pupils already at the school are the real experts, and should be able to help host such visits. They might also produce guides for Primary pupils, write letters to them about the school, or do a problem-solving 'surgery' in the Primary school. Homework itself is one of the biggest worries of prospective Secondary pupils, so if Secondary pupils can do a homework guide, for homework, they will be killing two birds with one stone, and developing their own understanding of homework techniques at the same time as helping improve the understanding of others.

A special event such as Work Experience can provide many good homework opportunities. Before the event, there is much preparatory work to be done, and this could include work on pupils' current Saturday or evening jobs, and surveys or analyses of the work done by members of the family or other adults in the neighbourhood. Following up the Work Experience, homework could be set on various aspects of work and school (stressing similarities and differences), and perhaps also producing advice for future participants.

- Information Technology and Homework.

Clearly, access to IT outside school is a difficulty when it comes to setting homework, although it is safe to assume that basic home computers will be as common as telephones, at least, in the next few years. With increasing standardisation of, or at least compatibility between, systems, though, and the development of IT facilities in homework centres and public libraries, pupils can be set some 'hands on' homework tasks. An audit of IT available to each pupil, useful in itself, might sensibly be done at regular intervals, to allow for such tasks to be set.

Searching the Internet is rewarding for every school subject, and can support almost any 'research' homework task. An interesting exercise could be to search on the Internet for help with homeworking itself: if pupils find the help (and I found 10 000 references in a couple of minutes, including study guides and motivational techniques), their achievement will be doubled.

As IT teaching should help pupils to become critical and largely autonomous users, homework tasks could be set that asked them to develop such skills. How could IT be used to support particular subjects or areas of life? What IT facilities would they like to see in libraries? Or, a question enjoyed more by pupils than teachers, will IT make teachers redundant? What problems could be caused by the storage of personal information on computers? The answers to these and similar questions could be put together in class, and used as the basis of surveys. Surveys, containing 'agree/disagree' responses to several statements, could then be carried out for another homework.

A pet hate of mine is seeing pupils using computers but working at the speed of an asthmatic ant, simply because they can't touch-type. If teachers can only get pupils to practice touch typing, on a regular basis during their early years in Secondary school (or earlier), then they will have my undying admiration. This should be done mainly as homework, though with tests of progress in class, and can be done with computers or if necessary with a sheet of paper with the keyboard drawn on it.

Whenever IT lessons are to cover information-handling exercises, pupils can use the homework time to collect the relevant information. The more important and useful the information, the better, and the tasks should also be tied in to other school subjects. To make the exercise more complete, the forms on which the data is to be collected could themselves be designed and produced in class on computers.

In many universities, it is a requirement of coursework that it be produced using IT. This makes the coursework easier to mark than handwritten work, but it also gives students an incentive to work on IT throughout the course. The same condition may well be put on GCSE and A Level coursework, and asking that pupils do homework in every subject, using computers, would be good preparation for this.

CHAPTER 13

Coursework and examinations

Coursework and exams play an increasing role in Primary as well as Secondary schools. Yet setting 'revision' homework, and setting up and monitoring coursework, at any level, worries many teachers. The need for an organised, balanced, approach is obvious when we think of the pressures on pupils, especially those doing GCSEs. Coursework for a GCSE pupil may involve 20 000 words (made up of half a dozen pieces at 3000 to 4000 words and some shorter pieces), at the same time as preparation for exams, and five hours a day of lessons. This is, for conscientious pupils, a greater pressure than they are likely to get later in their lives. For example, most pupils doing three A Levels with coursework will do about 15 000 words, along with exams and around three hours a day of lessons; post-graduate teacher training courses often have an expectation of 10 000 to 15 000 words, with few 'lessons' and no exam. The pressures of such work can be reduced if teachers have a coordinated approach to homework, supporting independent learning as well as simply spreading out the deadlines. The pressures on teachers, too, who are held accountable for grades achieved, can be reduced: if teachers do their best to support their pupils' progress, at least they can each say 'I did my best' (and 'I did my best for those pupils who failed or got low grades, as well as for those who got good grades'), and this should relieve some, just some, of the stress.

Coursework

Parents often complain about GCSE coursework keeping their offspring up all hours of the night before deadline day. Sometimes this is a problem with pupils' personal organisation, sometimes with the organisational skills of teachers or the school. It is important, when 'teaching' coursework, to be able to split the work into small enough sections, each with its own deadline, so that, should pupils get behind with their work, they will know this at an early date. By breaking the tasks down — for example into ideas, hypothesis, plans for the rest of the coursework, introduction, content, conclusion, evaluation — the teacher can also give regular feedback that will influence the rest of the coursework. The quality of teacher feedback is what makes the biggest difference to coursework, and when I've been a coursework examiner, I've been surprised at how much I could tell about the quality of the teachers' feedback from reading only the final product. One way of helping teachers coordinate work across the school, and support a 'break-up' of coursework tasks, is for the school to produce a single coursework guide, on offer at the start of Year 10 and shown to parents and carers at every Parents Evening, which not only lists the final deadlines for every subject with coursework, but the intermediate deadlines too. Some students will never meet deadlines, for all kinds of reasons, but the more information is given out, early, and to families as well as pupils, the more chances pupils have of getting themselves organised.

Here is a coursework survival guide, adapted from various leaflets and books. It should be adapted again, in any school that wishes to use it, after having been tested out on pupils and teachers from different disciplines.

- *Mission impossible?* There's plenty to do, but don't ignore any of your work in the hope that it will go away and self destruct. Whatever work you do, will improve the marks and grades, so however impossible perfection is, improvement is always possible.
- *As time goes by?* Take responsibility for your time. Time goes by whether you take responsibility or not: if you don't take responsibility for it, it will hurt you. The school takes weeks to write a timetable, to help the school run smoothly, and it covers hundreds of pupils and dozens of teachers. Writing your own coursework and revision timetable is so much easier. Having a timetable that you have decided yourself is best, as no one else can make you fit their timetable, unless you agree with it. If you don't want to do much work, write a timetable that reflects this — many pupils who do little work still spend a lot of time worrying about (not doing) their work. If you do want to work hard, you can write a timetable to reflect this, that also allows you to have some fun. An average week of lessons is 25 hours. If you do 15 hours a week homework (the maximum I've seen recommended by schools for pupils right up to A Levels), that adds up to 40 hours' work a week. A lot, perhaps, but there's enough hours in the week to do 40 hours' work, go out every evening, watch the television and videos, have hobbies and friends, and eat and sleep. People have worked 40-hour weeks for years, so if you want to work hard, give yourself a timetable that gets you working this number of hours and allows you plenty of time off. Sometimes, with really stressed pupils, I

82

82

recommend that they come to me with a 'leisure' timetable: a list of all the times in the week when they eat, sleep, and have fun. Then, the rest of the time, they can fill in with studying. A strange idea, maybe, but it works, by making pupils feel less guilty about having a rest, and more rested when it comes to study times.

- *Deadlines are unpleasant creatures.* They hang around in the shadows, occasionally calling out to you, but you just hope you haven't heard them. Being left alone in the shadows, they get hungrier and hungrier, until, eventually, they pounce on you, sink their teeth in and give you cold sweats and sleepless nights. Soon after this, they die peacefully, leaving you feeling bloodless and drained. Will you meet them again? Will you feed them, when they ask for food, or will you let them grow hungry again, so hungry they will attack you and bleed you dry? Deadlines are perfectly fair: if you feed them steadily through the year, they won't ask for any more food than if you let them get hungry: you just won't feel so bad yourself. You choose. Feed a deadline steadily, or wait nervously while it gets hungrier and more vicious.
- In general, no-one ever thanks you for completing work. You will have to thank yourself: get yourself a reward.

Exams

Exams have a long history at the centre of school life. They are stressful and often described as unfair, but the pressures of coursework have led some back to thinking exams may after all be a valuable form of assessment. Whatever public exams are taken, exams should be seen by pupils as reasonably 'normal'. This means setting tests, or using exam-style questions, regularly enough to make them familiar for pupils. When tests are used, it is important to use them to set targets: pupils should use results as the basis of further work, perhaps analysing or repeating at home important aspects of the test. ALIS information produced by Newcastle University, linking different exam results, is a good model for target-setting. The targets will need to be specific to the pupil, of course, but also specific to the exam syllabus: it is no good setting general 'learning' targets that do not help with the exams to be taken. Giving free access to syllabuses, and to exam papers, can make pupils be, and feel, much more responsible for their own progress.

Here is a revision guide, with the warning that, although 'revision tips' are popular, these are generally ignored, and a pupil approaching GCSE exams will often be given 10 or 11 different, contradictory, sets of revision tips, by 10 or 11 teachers. If ideas in here are found useful, adapt them to your purposes, and ask your pupils, and former pupils, whether the guide is useful and what could be added.

- *Why revise?* Revision improves grades: it's easy to throw away two years' work for a few hours' revision. Write down why you think you should revise, including all the things you want out of exams, such as jobs or places on courses. Be as clear and detailed as you can, and don't even think about lying: your teacher won't be impressed, and it won't help you in the end. If you don't want to pass exams, then you don't have any reason to revise. But we've never yet found anyone like this.
- *What with?* Notes (done as you go along), syllabuses, revision guides, textbooks. Make a list, for homework, of all the resources you now have, for this subject, and all the resources you can realistically get, before the exam. Don't assume that something helpful for another pupil is also helpful for you: work out what *you* need. For difficult written exams, one of the things you may need is a list of words they use in the exam, so, to start off your list of useful resources, here's my list of useful words and their meanings:

  Analyse = examine in detail each part and show the relationship of the parts to the whole; assess = estimate the value or the importance; compare = state the similarities, differences can be noted, but similarities should be emphasised; contrast = state the differences; define = give the meaning of; describe = tell in detail; discuss = examine the different sides of the debate, and present the whole case; explain = state how and why it happens or how to do it; criticise or critique = examine and judge; evaluate = examine the importance of the problem, pointing out the advantages and disadvantages; examine = investigate the detail; explain = give reasons for; illustrate = use examples or figures to explain; interpret = explain the meaning; justify = give reasons that support the argument or action; outline = indicate the essential points; relate = show the connections; summarise = make a brief statement covering the necessary points.
- *When?* As you go along, then, following a timetable. If you don't work for 18 months, revision will actually be 'first vision': this is difficult. If you work as you go along, and keep your notes and handouts reasonably well organised, revision will be natural and easy. If you are reading this, and it is already too late, never mind, but if you are reading this early in the course, remember, in 18 months time, that we told you so! A timetable is not extra work, it is a way of putting the work together. Not having a timetable is like having a pile of bricks. Having a timetable is like having a house. When thinking about a timetable, think about when you actually work (not when you pretend to work) and when you want to work. Of all the hours' work you put in, try to organise them so that you balance your revision between

different subjects, and don't leave any big gaps. Now, write a 'timetable' of the work you did last week, decide whether that was a good use of your time, and write a timetable for next week. Next week, look back at the timetable and see if it worked: if it worked, good, if not, change it until you get a timetable that works for you!

- *How?* Decide what conditions help you work, and make the most of them. Some people like noise and people around them, to help them work, some people like quiet isolation. Some want plenty of food, others rely on coffee. There are pupils who need to work in short bursts of 10 or 20 minutes, with a little rest, others can work for two or three hours at a time. Work out, for yourself, what is best — but don't kid yourself, don't say 'I like listening to music when I work' but actually you just like listening to music and always forget the work! When you've got the conditions right, think about how to revise. There are two kinds of task: easy, 'mechanical', tasks like sorting your notes out, or underlining the important bits in your files; and difficult, 'learning', tasks like memorising quotations. However you work, remember that you should give your brain a chance to recover, so alternate the 'mechanical' and the 'learning' tasks. Beyond that, I can't tell you much: you need to write down, here, how to revise your subjects, given the amount of work you've already done. You are the expert: you've done enough exams before, and you should have learned from them!

- *Don't panic.* Panic is nature's way of getting you prepared for something important. It is natural to feel panicky. If you *don't* feel panicky, there's probably something wrong, so just don't worry about panicking. Remember, too, that an hour's work is better for you than an hour's panicking: if you are feeling like a panic, do an hour's work. It is surprisingly difficult to work and panic at the same time.

CHAPTER 14

Teachers doing their own homework: Organising your own professional development and study

This chapter and Chapter 18, on managers' homework, are complementary, as all members of the profession have much in common, especially their homework. Teachers do 'homework' every week: an average teacher does around 52 hours a week of work, and perhaps 40 % of this is done at home. Homework can be organised more efficiently, but there are also wider issues of professional development and study. This will I hope have a value in itself, but I'm covering the topic also because teachers who are aware of the difficulties of doing their own homework, should be better able to set, monitor and support the homework of their pupils.

I've often asked teachers, and pupils, to write down how much work they do each day for the next week. They are very reluctant to do this: I've sometimes resorted to asking people to estimate what they have done in the previous week. Even then, they are reluctant to do the exercise, and even more reluctant to say what they have written down. If pushed, they may say how many hours they've worked, but only if prefaced by 'but this was nothing like the week before, when I was up all night doing reports'. My only explanation for the reluctance to say exactly how many hours are worked, is that teachers would rather 'feel' overworked than 'know' they work a certain number of hours. This is partly to do with the fact that many people (including, especially, the pupils, the school's managers, and the government) think teachers can or should do more. As teachers are told they are not doing enough, they have to tell themselves they are doing 'too much'. My advice would be to work out what you (or your unions) think is reasonable (and 52 hours a week seems more than reasonable), and make sure that you do that. Any changes in your work, once you've settled on a 'reasonable' number of hours, should involve rearranging, not increasing, the work. As a recent advertisement said: 'work smarter, not harder'. Keep a diary of the work you do for one week. If it is over 52 hours (or whatever is decided as a reasonable number), work out what you could stop doing, or what you could do quicker. If you can't stop any of the tasks, or can't do any quicker, then keep a diary for *another* week. If this second week is also over 52 hours, then find a job outside teaching: teaching is too hard for you. If, in the first week of the diary, you do much *less* than 52 hours, then keep very quiet, smile to yourself, and don't tell your colleagues. You are happy.

Teachers' homework is difficult enough, yet thousands of teachers want to add to the work, by completing courses, diplomas or degrees. This may be ambition working: qualifications can help with promotion. It may also be curiosity and the wish to continue the learning that got them into teaching in the first place. Teachers are expected to learn new syllabuses, ways of teaching or assessing, forms of organisation, so it is not surprising that they should want to get some formal credit for work that they do. All of this is healthy. What implications does it have for teachers' homework? First, make even more sure that you work out how many hours of teaching work would be reasonable, as above, and stick to that. Second, remember everything you say to your pupils about their work, and say it to yourself. Tutors and supervisors of MAs and PhDs say to their students things like 'just tell me, what exactly are you trying to say here?', or 'I'm not clear whether you are quoting here or paraphrasing', or 'is there any evidence for what you say?' These same phrases are all used by teachers, talking to pupils doing GCSEs and A Levels. So, whatever you tell pupils, about methods of working, pacing themselves, being clear, getting work done by deadlines, or whatever, tell yourself, as these are the same problems you are likely to come up against.

There used to be something of a gap between the images of teaching and research, with teaching seeing itself as 'practical' and research being seen as 'theoretical'. The gap, or perceived gap, has been reduced, as teachers have been expected to do more and more work on policies and the application of policies, and as research has looked more and more at issues such as 'school improvement' and 'reading recovery'. Happily, this coming together has meant that teachers doing courses are more likely to be able to justify their work to their colleagues, and are more likely to be able to make use of their work in school, in completing assignments. Initial teacher training has moved in the same direction, with school-based coursework, including school-based research, being the norm. Some have recommended that educational research should be more like medical research, with everyday professional activities being used systematically as evidence for professional research and development.

One big, growing, area of professional development is involvement in school-based teacher training. We all learn by teaching, and so we can learn about teaching by teaching student teachers. The kind of mentoring and tutoring that schools are now expected to provide for student teachers is much more detailed, and much harder work, than the older style of looking after students. This can be seen as a problem, but it is also an opportunity to gain new skills and knowledge. One of the topsy-turvy consequences of introducing a National Curriculum so quickly, is that student teachers often teach their mentors (if the mentors trained before 1988) more about the subtleties of the system than vice versa. A more straightforward opportunity is for mentors to gain qualifications in mentoring, and such qualifications should help careers in more practical ways than some more abstract subjects. Such 'homework' lies snugly with on-going professional development, then.

Whatever homework you do, try to balance the home and school work in such a way that neither suffers. If homework is so demanding that school work suffers, or the other way around, then a re-adjustment is probably needed. It is a delicate balance, as it is very likely that a teacher doing a part time MA will have less time to do school work, yet in the longer term, the school work should benefit. Again, I'd advise thinking about how we would deal with an enthusiastic pupil. Most teachers recognise the point at which enthusiasm or over-commitment in a pupil leads to all areas of their work suffering. Try the same diagnosis on yourself.

Part 3
A Managers' Guide to Homework

CHAPTER 15

Developing policies and practices in departments

Many of the policies developed and implemented by managers come up against problems of perspective. From the manager's point of view, the whole school is generally seen as benefiting from consistency, with consistency being maintained by creating and monitoring policies. Teachers, on the other hand, tend to see whole-school consistency as reducing the importance of individual professional judgment, and as weakening the influence of departments. This is a common problem with whole-school homework policies. The more specific the policy is (e.g. 'set homework once a week'), the more individual teachers and departments will protest, either by trying to change the policy as it is being made, or, more commonly, by ignoring the policy once it has been passed. The more vague or general the policy is (e.g. 'homework is a good thing'), the less able it is to have any effect. One strategy for avoiding these problems is to concentrate on helping departments to develop their own policies.

- Managers should be midwives, helping at the birth of written policies, not conceiving the policies themselves. I like to think of policies as existing whether they are written down or not: every department is pregnant with policies, if they haven't been written down yet. The job of 'developing policies' should be about finding out what is being done at present (the current policy, whether written down or not), and supporting or improving that practice. Too many teachers are good at what they do, but give a poor impression of themselves because their good practice is not recorded (they have no written policies), or their formal, written, policy is so much worse than their actual practice. Managers can help make the policies explicit and more relevant to the work of the whole school, as described below.
- As a consultant, one of my favourite jobs is going into a school, reading about the whole-school aims and policies, and talking to heads of departments about what they do and how they work. A couple of

days later, I'll go in with my account of what a head of department has said, related to whole-school policies: this takes the form of a set of departmental policies. Every time I've done this, so far, the head of department has said something like 'this looks really good: do you mean these are what my department's policies should look like?' I generally reply that these are what the department's policies really are, whatever it says in the departmental handbook. One happy head of department. Like a good therapist, a good consultant simply repeats back to the client what the client tells them, in such a way that the client thinks the consultant has come up with really good advice. In fact, the advice is only good because it is what the client does anyway, but don't tell any of my clients that! In any case, the work of 'bringing out' policies can just as well be done by a manager.

- When developing homework policies, it is useful to look at the financial and timetabling implications of the policies. For example, departments choosing between textbooks and worksheets may choose the latter, to enable more effective homework to be set, and departments wanting new computers may be asked what access pupils will have to them outside lesson time.

- A small minority of teachers don't set homework, or don't care whether pupils complete it. However, a much larger number will say that, whatever homework policy is decided, there will be pupils who do no homework. Some managers might say, 'well, it's your job to make sure they do homework', but this seems a little harsh. If there are pupils unable to do homework, this is an issue about access to education, and therefore about equal opportunities and, generally, special needs.

- Departmental, as opposed to whole-school, policies need to have the flavour of that department and that subject. All the 'subject' chapters in this book include some reference to the special role of homework for that subject, a role that justifies homework. Departmental policies should include such references. Managers should encourage individuality within departments, whilst at the same time promoting whole-school goals.

- It seems reasonable to ask departments what they would like in a 'homework centre', and what generic homework tasks in their departments could be collected by the school. Again, this is a way of promoting departmental responsibility for their own areas, whilst helping whole-school initiatives. Even thinking about homework centres can help departments to realise how they might improve their homework practices.

CHAPTER 16

Developing whole-school policies

The previous chapter looked at how departmental policies could be developed with the help of managers. There is still a need for work on whole-school policies, and, beyond this, LEA policies for schools wishing to work as part of a larger team. Whole-school policies are only helpful if they add something to the work of departments: there is little point in the policies contradicting each other or being identical except for the substitution of the school's name for that of the department. Two areas that can be distinctive to a whole-school homework policy are those of coordination, and of institutional and community support.

• A good homework policy for a school will explain how the homework demands of different departments will be balanced. This means more than just working out a homework timetable — though a timetable is very useful. It means giving guidance on how homework tasks can complement each other, and how they should be coordinated. Homework in Year 7, for example, should be helpful in getting pupils used to new learning styles, and informing parents and carers about how they can help with children's work: in Chapter 12 I've written about organising a coordinated set of Year 7 homework tasks, for the first few weeks of the year. Year 9 homework should stress preparation for the styles of work used in GCSE courses, while GCSE homework is likely to need particular care and coordination. A whole-school policy would be useful on coursework deadlines, support given at home, who to approach if pupils are overworked or underworked, and much else. It is surprising to me that some schools give no overall timings for homework, not saying how much should be done each week, in different years. Even more schools have an idea of appropriate timings, but don't publicise this. So many arguments between home and school could be resolved by the school saying 'We will set this number of hours of homework a week. If your child does less than this, then either they are doing too little work or our teachers have forgotten the school's policy. Either way, please let us know.'

- A whole-school homework policy should explain how the school can formally support homework. This may include a whole-school language policy that means pupils get a more consistent response to their work, or practical support such as libraries. How is the library used, or other learning resources? What about computers: are any on loan, or available outside school hours, and are any recommended for home use? Are there any special revision sessions in the holidays or weekends before important exams? Are public libraries recommended, and when are they available? Are particular reference books, especially dictionaries, recommended?

- Yet there are important ethical issues that should be addressed. I've recommended many forms of 'engaging' homework, in which pupils will ask question outside school, describe features of their home lives, and so on. A school policy can clarify the ethics of homework, and avoid problems associated with uncontrolled but engaging homework tasks. For example, I would say that pupils should not be asked to do street surveys on their own or unsupervised. All tasks done outside the house should be set with care, and if necessary, permission should be sought from home, and alternative tasks offered to reluctant pupils. Information about families that might be embarrassing should not be sought, and if offered should not be made available to other pupils. When it comes to formal GCSE or A Level coursework, it is worth publicising exam board guidance on issues such as plagiarism. The school can publicise these regulations more effectively than individual teachers, and there is, in any case, a continuum from 'copying' and other forms of 'cheating' in lower school homework tasks, to plagiarism and failure to acknowledge quotations.

- Other people who can generate policies are pupils and parents or carers. A policy developed by teachers, pupils and their families will carry more weight. Managers should be responsible for bringing these people together, and they can continue the links, organising (or delegating the organisation of) book stalls or course guides or special events for all concerned with the school. The events will be informative, but will also give people a chance to inform you. Listening to complaints may sometimes be painful, but that's part of the job, and as long as people complain to you, at least they still think you're worth complaining to. Communication, therefore, is vital. For regular communication, most schools have homework diaries. Where these diaries are used, they should be monitored, not in a punitive way, but in order to see how effective they are and how they can be made more effective. Pupils could help design the diaries, and should certainly be allowed to talk about how they are used.

CHAPTER 17

Partnerships with parents and the community

Schools rightly stress the educational role of parents and other members of, and organisations within, the local community. This can be the start of a creative partnership between schools, parents and the community. Occasionally, though, it sounds as if the school is making an excuse — blaming parents or poverty for underachievement. There are indeed good reasons why pupils of similar abilities, but from different backgrounds, are likely to achieve at different levels, and schools cannot wholly 'compensate' for social inequalities. Yet every study of schools also recognises that schools can make *some* difference, and that different schools, or different teachers within the same schools, can affect pupils in different ways. Some of the more subtle studies went further. They looked at why an environmental factor might affect pupils' achievement, and how schools could address specific problems. In Strathclyde (the local authority, now abolished, responsible for Glasgow and a huge area beyond), the Social Services sector came to the reasonable conclusion that poverty at home might disadvantage children at school, as children from such homes might have fewer facilities to help with homework, and so on. In order to reduce the 'cycle of poverty', that is, children of poor backgrounds being consigned to adult poverty, the authority funded homework centres in schools in relatively poor areas. This acknowledged that schools were not entirely passive when it came to environmental influences on their pupils. Similarly, when it comes to parents and carers, schools have an obligation to try to address any issues that may affect the progress of their children. A simple example would be the fact, often told to me as though nothing could be done about it, that some parents themselves have difficulties with basic literacy and numeracy skills. Only a few schools, of those ready to blame the underachievement of pupils on parents, have thought seriously about offering classes or advice to parents in basic skills. Some schools are great at this, having special events for parents and carers where they can find out about the skills that would help them support their children's education. Others encourage parents to join classes, alongside pupils. At Parents Evenings, schools may provide good, clear, information about what resources are available, and they may provide interpreters for parents less skilled in English. In these and many other ways, the educational role of parents and other carers can be acknowledged and enhanced. Building a partnership may go even further.

Partnerships imply a group of people with similar powers getting together with a single aim. Parents, carers and schools do indeed have similar power in the important sense that all are responsible for their children's upbringing. The legal role of schools is defined in terms of the role of parents: schools are *in loco parentis*, 'in the place of' parents, whilst the children are there. Yet schools can forget this, and assume that families can't be in an equal partnership with schools, as schools are filled with the experts, whilst families are not. I prefer to look at the issue another way around. There are about 140 000 hours in 16 years. Expert or not, families are responsible for bringing up children for approximately 125 000 hours, up to the age of 16, whilst schools are responsible for the remaining 15 000 hours. Whatever schools think, families are more involved in bringing up their children than schools are: in terms of hours, they are over eight times as 'responsible'. Even more than this, children will have learnt more in the years before school begins than they will ever learn for the rest of their lives, and they will spend far more time outside than in school during their 'schooldays'. So schools are indeed in an unequal partnership, because they have such a small amount of power or influence, comparatively speaking. Getting into an 'equal' partnership with parents and carers is a privilege for schools.

The kind of practical partnerships that schools can build will depend on the circumstances of the school and its community. Examples of interesting partnerships include ways of extending the school into the home, for example through the impressively sensible PACT and IMPACT schemes (helping with primary reading and maths), in which tasks are set that necessarily involve 'helpers' at home. There are also ways of bringing the home into the school, as when parents produce tapes of their favourite stories, in their home languages, for use in schools. A third, more radical, approach is based on more 'political' models of power-sharing, as when families are fully involved with education and other services, generating policies and strategies for implementing them. An important aspect of school-family partnerships, too easily forgotten, is that the adults most likely to be heavily involved in supporting their children's education are women — mothers and grandmothers, especially — so 'empowering' families generally means empowering women. Schools, can easily make assumptions about what 'good' mothers 'should' do (I've heard parents of primary children complain most about this), and can give undue weight to the 'authoritative' views expressed by relatively uninvolved men in families (I've heard parents of secondary pupils complain most about this).

There are three stages in building partnerships with parents.

- Recognising the skills, understanding, commitment and (even if you don't believe all that) responsibility of parents and carers for the upbringing (education, in the broadest sense) of children.
- Providing realistic opportunities for parents and carers to help their children with their school work. This may include homework diaries, schemes requiring work to be done with helpers at home, or classes or advice for parents on improving their own basic skills. Being realistic means realising that there is no quick fix for all problems.
- Promoting and participating in shared initiatives, perhaps with other organisations and services, in which schools and families can work together to create more opportunities for children. 'Sharing' doesn't sit well with a lot of rules and regulations, with punishments or contracts when people break these rules. It should be a positive approach, based on an assumption that everyone wants the children to be successful and happy.

I believe that initiatives such as homework centres have proved good examples of all three of these strategies. More about that, though, in Chapter 28.

CHAPTER 18

Managers doing their own homework: Organising your own professional development and study

Managers are teachers, too, and this chapter must complement Chapter 14, on teachers doing their own homework. There are, however, some special characteristics of managers, that will affect what and how they learn. Managing a school means taking a whole-school perspective, unlike heads of department and other post-holders who will have sectional interests and will want to 'fight their corner'. This means that managers' homework, too, will be likely to be about the whole school. This is not a criticism of the different perspectives, as both are needed, but a recognition of the separate identities of sub-groups within a school, with distinct interests and contributions to make. A second distinctive feature of managers is that they are likely do more 'new' homework (not necessarily more *work*) than any other group of teachers after qualification. They are likely to experience the biggest change in their jobs, on becoming managers, and will usually continue taking on new initiatives and responsibilities for the rest of their time in post. A third feature of managers' lives is that they may find it hardest to organise their time, because the demands of the job are so complex and amorphous. Here is some advice.

● Distinguish daily chores from your long-term tasks, and don't be tempted to let all homework be short-term. If all your homework seems to involve dealing with short-term issues, then at least make sure that your work is cumulative, and therefore has long-term uses. Each short-term solution should be the basis for solving the next short-term problem. A simple illustration is that of a manager having to look up the Health and Safety regulations, because someone is making a claim against the school after an accident. This 'homework' (if it is done as homework) will, if done thoroughly, be useful when the next claim is made. It could also be the basis of a longer-term review of the school's health and safety policy. In this way, short-term work is cumulative and leads in to long-term work.

- Managers are in general responsible for large-scale changes in a school, and are often fighting against other groups in the school who may want things to stay the same or to control changes themselves. Change should be based on knowledge and understanding, and this means research, or homework. The most obvious basis of research is the school itself, and school managers often have a ready-made structure for doing this research, with regular and systematic INSET for experienced staff, and induction and support systems for new and student teachers in the school. Pupils and parents can be 'surveyed' too, and are readily available. I would recommend that INSET, in particular, is used for such research and development work, and not for simply telling teachers what to do. Imaginative managers will tie this research into other forms of research, including degree and other qualifications. I get upset when I see managers lacking the confidence to use INSET in this way (for example by only ever inviting speakers from outside the school), or telling, not asking, staff about changes.
- Qualifications, such as MAs, MBAs, or PhDs, are popular with managers or those on the edge of being managers. They are substantial homework tasks, and are useful for careers. Don't do them, though, if they take your mind off the job. It is easy to say 'I'll coast through my MA as best I can', but it too easily takes over. Qualifications are best if they are related to your specific job – for example, an MA on assessment if you are responsible for assessment – and if they are mostly based in your own school. School-based research, more popular in recent years, is worth shopping around for.
- Managers tend to be given opportunities to go on lots of short courses, providing more homework, or at least out-of-school work. It may seem obvious, but I will still say that you should only go on these if they are useful to you and the school; it is a little less obvious, that you should only go on these if they are going to be *used*. A course on differentiation may be useful, but if there are no opportunities to make use of it in school, don't go. My test of such courses is to ask whether you will fight to talk to other staff about the issues at the next staff meeting or INSET session. If you are feeling shy, the course will be a waste of your homework time.
- Part of a manager's homework is, or should be, learning the next job up. Some say that the sign of future leaders is that they are always thinking about how they would do the job better than the current leader. This is true of the teaching profession (except that in teaching, *everyone* thinks they can do better than the Head), and a manager should expect to be doing some critical analysis of the work of those higher up the system.

Part 4
A Parents' Guide to Homework

CHAPTER 19

Introduction: 'Homework is Hell'

There have been several newspaper articles about homework, with titles like 'homework is hell' or 'why homework is too much of a bad thing'. There is either too much or too little homework, it is too difficult or too easy; it spoils hobbies or social activities or it fails to keep the children off the streets. Homework is the most common cause of educational arguments between parents and children, parents and teachers, and children and teachers. I know, homework can be hell. In both hell and heaven, I was told in a school assembly, the knives, forks and spoons are too long to feed yourself with; the *difference* between hell and heaven is that in hell, you starve, but in heaven, you feed each other. This whole book is about how to feed each other, how teachers can set good homework for pupils, how school managers can help teachers pupils and parents, and how parents can work with children and schools to support education.

This section of the book, and the shorter guide for parents in Chapter 33, are not guides to bringing up children, but guides to supporting school work and homework. There are two approaches, one about being generally supportive of your child's education, and the other about giving detailed practical help. The approaches are complementary, but you may feel more comfortable with one or the other, and your choice will be affected by what your child wants or needs. Incidentally, although I write here about 'parents', I am writing for all who care for children — parents, grandparents, sisters and brothers, other relatives, professional carers, and anyone else left holding the 'baby'. In those sections of the book addressed to teachers, I've referred to 'parents and carers', because teachers often forget that children can be looked after by many people. In this section, however, I've just referred to 'parents', on the grounds that, if you are a grandparent reading this book, you are hardly likely to forget the fact. I hope all carers will feel included, even if I don't always name you.

Being supportive

Parents of Primary pupils often compete against each other, and not just in 'parents' races' on Sports Day. Children may be set a homework task of making a Roman shield: all the shields will be made by the parents, who will compete ruthlessly to make the best one. As children get older, homework gets harder. There is a whole set of traumas of dedicated parents having to work on almost impossible homework tasks, requiring trips to stationers and libraries, phone calls to other parents 'expert' in particular subjects, and impossible standards barely met by the combined efforts of whole families. So homework is often parent-work, and yet the biggest complaint about homework, from parents, is that there should be more of it. Like castor oil, the fact that it is so unpleasant is taken as evidence that it is good for you. What I recommend are ways of supporting homework that don't require of parents a lot of time or work. I was upset when, as a young teacher, an inspector preferred the lesson in which I wandered around the room, helping the pupils with their work, to the lesson in which I gave a fascinating lecture full of arm waving and eloquent words. In fact, as the inspector said, the first lesson was better because the pupils were learning more. The same goes for parental support for homework. Don't be tempted to think being supportive always means hard work: it isn't the amount of work you do that matters, but the amount of learning your child does. 'Leave well alone' is often good advice – though parents of adolescents hardly need to be told of that already tempting strategy.

All parents value education, and want their children to do well, but there are ways of showing how much you value education that can help children do even better. By doing courses – evening classes, correspondence courses, or simply following educational series on the television – you show that education is useful and interesting, something for a lifetime and not just a burden on childhood. By getting involved with your child's school, attending shows and Parents Evenings and also helping with classes or joining the governing body, you show that the school is to be taken seriously. By asking your child about their school work and homework, even if they answer with little more than 'okay' or 'boring', you show that you have at least thought about their education. All three of these activities (doing courses, getting involved in school, and asking about your child's work) are also helpful in themselves, and shouldn't be done just out of a sense of duty. Enjoy them all and then, if they don't help your child, at least you'll have had some fun.

All parents love and value their children, though we all know a few who have strange ways of showing it. It can help, however, if we separately value 'the child' and their 'intelligence', abilities or achievements. Tell them what you think of them as children, and not just what you think of them as learners. And if they don't do so well at school, still tell them how much you think of them as children and how proud you are of all their good qualities. Children are likely to feel more secure, and be able to do more, if they *know* that people who care for them will value them even if they fail at school, as well as taking pleasure in their successes at school. The same is helpful at home as at school. Experienced teachers often say to a pupil who has misbehaved 'I know that you are thoughtful and kind, so what happened here?' The pupil is likely to be better behaved for that teacher, and is more likely to admit their 'crime', than if the teacher says 'you are a thoughtless and unkind person, behaving in this way'. Similarly, a pupil is more likely to respond well to 'this work is not as good as it might be, for someone of your intelligence' or 'this work is brilliant, and shows how clever you are', than 'this work shows how stupid you are' or 'this work is brilliant, considering how stupid you are'. Intelligence, anyway, is a bit of a funny business, and it doesn't help to think of it as fixed and unalterable. Whether or not there is such a thing as a fixed intelligence (and psychologists have argued about this for years), intelligence is best thought of as being like the power or engine-size of a car. Big engines may make cars go faster on test tracks, but in London, where I live, as in most of this country, having a 'powerful' car is not what makes the difference between getting around faster or slower. Knowing the streets, going at the right time or knowing when jams are likely, make far more difference. It's the same with 'intelligence'. It isn't how 'powerful' it is, but what is done with it. There are plenty of Porsche drivers still stuck in traffic long after I've got home in my Golf, just as there are plenty of people with more 'raw' intelligence than your child whom your child will leave far behind!

Studying takes a lot of energy. People can feel as drained and exhausted after completing an essay as after doing an aerobics session. The happier and more contented children are, the more energy they will have to study. The more unhappy or stressed they are, the harder it will be to concentrate on studying. Ironically, parents can at times put so much pressure on their children to do well at school, that they are so stressed that learning becomes impossible. I've taught many older pupils, especially, in this position. It's a no-win situation, I know, as there are probably as many pupils who find homework difficult because their families 'just don't care'. I would just go back to what I said earlier, that parents shouldn't think that they are being more helpful the more work they put in: all that parents want is happy and successful children.

Practical help

Parents usually feel confident helping with Primary school work, because they know the answers. When it comes to Secondary school, the first thing to say is that you don't need to know the answers. If you do know the answers, it won't be very helpful, in the long run, to tell your child, as they won't be doing the learning. If you don't know the answers, you can help by telling your children how clever they are to be able to do such things that you don't understand! There are four practical stages of help that you can give.

- Getting started is often the hardest part of doing homework. We all tend to put difficult things off, and then find that, when we get round to it, it wasn't so difficult after all. The same goes for homework. Some books say that children should have a rest after school, and only start homework later in the evening; others recommend doing homework immediately after school, and may even set up a place in school that encourages such timing. For children who find getting started easy, a rest is probably helpful, but for children who are chronic 'putters off', it is probably better to get the 'getting started' over as soon as possible, and have a regular, fixed, routine. In the same way, it is often better to start with the least-liked subject, if that will avoid worrying during more favoured homework tasks. Talk to your child about this. It took me years, until I was in my 30s, to realise that I didn't mind working: what had made me anxious all these years was waiting for the work to start. Help your child to recognise the difference between worrying about homework and worrying about getting started.

- Finding a space is the next task. Some books, and lots of furniture stores, will try to persuade you that every child needs a desk, a bookcase, an angle-poise lamp, and a chair that swivels, all in a separate room. For many children, this would indeed be ideal, though a few do prefer working on a kitchen table, with people and food all around, or in front of the television, with something bland to watch when the work gets boring. You will only know, again, by asking your child what sort of place is the best for him or her. Then, you may be able to make that place a little bit better. Putting in a higher wattage light bulb, or getting a pet-proof large plastic box in which to keep school books, are likely to be as helpful as converting the attic into the Reading Room of the British Museum. Similarly, getting the whole family to agree to leave the kitchen alone between 4.00 and 5.30, or to avoid annoying the 'homeworker' during those hours, should be easier than banning all contact with them for their entire teenage years. Pupils frequently say that the thing that most stops them doing homework is younger brothers and sisters being annoying. Arranging an acceptable space and time for homework is more realistic than expecting brothers and sisters to be permanently considerate. Remember, too, and remind your child, that the best place for your child's homework might not be at home at all, but at the school library at lunchtime, or a public library after school, or a friend's house. It isn't 'cheating' to do homework in school, as long as it is well done.

- Doing the homework itself comes next. Asking questions is generally more helpful than answering them. In class, teachers will start the lesson by explaining what the pupil should do, and will spend a lot of the rest of the lesson reminding pupils about what they have already said. When a pupil says 'what should I do?', inexperienced teachers may repeat the instructions over and over; more experienced teachers are likely to ask 'what did I say earlier?' or 'what does it say in the book?' or 'what do you think you should do?'. The same technique is good for parents, too, especially as they are less likely to know exactly what the child should be doing. Other ways of helping include offering to test your child, or being available to be drawn (for Art) or questioned (for History) or read to (for English). You might want to check the homework, for spelling or presentation. Remember, in all of this, that you are a parent and not a teacher. You will rarely be helpful if you try to 'teach' your child, as the child may simply find it confusing. I say that especially for parents who, during the day, are indeed teachers: try to switch off when you get home, and just be a parent.

  You may be able to offer more help if you know, in advance, what sort of topics your child will be doing. Schools are much better, now, at having clear, relatively fixed, plans for the whole year. Ask the school what topics are likely to come up, so that you can be better prepared to talk about the topics. If your child seems to have no homework, and you are determined that they do some, you could always try to get them to do one of the homework tasks from Chapters 5 to 12 of this book. However, a more gentle approach would be to ask your child to tell you about the most interesting things they've learned in a favourite subject.

- Finally, help your child be lazy. Of all the advice I've given in this book, this is probably the strangest, but I do think it important. Being idle means getting nothing done, and this is a bad thing. Being lazy, however, means enjoying doing nothing, or enjoying relaxing, and this is vital. Secondary school homework is usually recommended as lasting between 4 and 15 hours a week, depending on the age of the child and the amount of work done in school (ask the school if you want to know what they recommend). Even at the busiest times, your child should still have plenty of time to relax, or to do completely 'non-school' things. Instead, lots of pupils spend several years constantly worrying about work they should be doing, but not doing it or leaving it to the last minute. You can help your child by making sure they know the difference between five hours' worrying plus one hour's work, and one hour's work plus five hours' relaxing. This means stopping doing homework, after it is done, rather than spending the whole evening getting started. Help them relax, help them be lazy.

I'd like to end this introduction with a letter I got from a teacher. It is important that you know you are not alone!

"Dear Julian,

I was a parent long before I was a teacher, and purely from a parental point of view I hate homework. It has caused me no end of heartache with one of my children, who resists all attempts by me and his teachers to bribe him, cajole him, threaten detentions, or whatever else. He does do some homework, but it is usually only when he feels like it. On the other hand I have another child who is almost paranoid about it, and he comes home and ritualistically does all his homework the night it is set. He gets very distressed if anything interrupts his routine and he is unable to get straight on it. I am worried he will run out of steam before the end of his school career.

Homework serves to cause endless friction between concerned and caring parents and their teenage sons who would rather be doing something else. Or it causes concern when a child is at the opposite extreme and seems to spend an excessive amount of his free time engaged on it. I realise this is probably not what you are looking for, but I feel much better in my role as parent having got that off my chest. Regards."

CHAPTER 20

Supporting Reading, Writing and Oral skills

The National Curriculum says that all pupils will study English, and that they will also develop their communication skills in other subjects. Their work in English is assessed by looking at reading, writing, and oral skills — speaking and listening. Too many people forget, however, that children will have learnt more about language before they are five years old than any school will ever teach them, and most of that is down to you. Parents teach children how to speak and understand their language, and, as everyone knows who has tried to learn a second language, the first few months or years of learning a language are the hardest and the most rewarding. So if a teacher says that you are not helping much with English homework, you may be able to remind the teacher that it was you, and not a teacher, who did all the hard work.

You can still help your child progress through the English National Curriculum, though, and that is the point of this chapter. The general rule is that the more interest you take in reading, writing, speaking and listening, the more your child will learn. It doesn't make a big difference whether you were brought up speaking English yourself, or learnt it as a second language, or how well you did at school in the English lessons. And parents can help their children even if the children are better at the subject than the parents. Good football managers can still help players in their teams, even if the players are more skilful than the manager ever was. The same goes for helping your child with English, and it's not so different with the other subjects, either.

- Reading.
  Having almost any books around the house is going to help children with their reading, because the books will be familiar and therefore less off-putting for children, and the more books the better — the main limit being cost. You don't need to force the books on children. It may seem strange, but I get the impression that information in books 'seeps out': children seem to learn from books that they never seem to read.

Perhaps they read books when we aren't looking, or perhaps they get enough information from the writing and pictures on the cover and spine. Some children believe they learn how to read by 'magic'. Someone told me she used to sit in class, waiting all excited for her turn to read, because she thought that this time it would simply 'happen': sadly for her, it didn't.

When it comes to choosing which books are best left around the house, the rules are that you should find them enjoyable (and then your children may enjoy them), or useful (such as reference books), or that they are useful for the school work (and you will probably have to ask the school about these). Secondhand books are just as good as new books, although, when it comes to school books, there have been so many changes in recent years, that it is worth getting new or very nearly new ones. Libraries have, or can get, any books you may want, so if you are going to buy any, you can concentrate on the ones you think are most interesting or useful.

Some parents think that helping children with reading means stopping them reading 'bad' books. In general, unless children are reading positively dangerous or obscene books, you don't really need to worry. Don't stop them reading books, just add to the range of books they read. And remember that it isn't just what you read, but how you read it: if children are reading 'rubbish', they may know how bad the book is, and enjoy making fun of it, just like adults often enjoy criticising television programmes they think are 'rubbish'.

As well as books, other reading matter will also help children. Newspapers and magazines can be left lying around, and you can point out interesting or useful items. For some topics, it may be helpful to cut out and keep bits of newspapers: parents did a lot of that when there were special articles about the 50th anniversary of World War Two events.

An activity that will help you and your children, is to get them to read things for you. Forms, catalogues, holiday brochures, television guides, and instruction booklets, for example, could be good materials. You could pretend (if it is a pretence) that it is all too complicated for you to understand, or you could simply ask for help. Children can be asked to be dictionary or encyclopaedia experts for the family, to settle arguments or help when you're writing something important. Better still if you can get them to read you novels or other things.

Children may have a lot of difficulty reading, and if they are good at other subjects, this problem may be called 'dyslexia'. People who find reading easy, may not understand what this difficulty is like, and as a child I was very unsympathetic to my classmates who couldn't read very well. They found it just as difficult understanding why I couldn't swim, but it was only as an adult that I realised how similar the problems were. Non-swimmers and non-readers are not helped by being told how stupid or incompetent they are, and may turn their lack of skill into a major fear. If you think your children are having real difficulties reading, keep encouraging them, gently, and ask them what is important to them: a child who is desperately keen to read may welcome specialist help, one who is terrified may want to get on with other things for a while, and come back to reading when their confidence has increased. Whatever help they get for reading, they will need to be reminded how skilful or clever they are in other areas of their education. Famous people with reading difficulties that could be described as 'dyslexia' – either by their own accounts, or from evidence in their work, include Einstein, Leonardo da Vinci, Auguste Rodin, Michael Heseltine, Cher, and Susan Hampshire. Remind your children what impressive company they are in!

- Writing.
It used to be that the range of writing done in school was quite narrow: children were expected to write stories and later, essays, along with a few summaries and exercises. Now, although these are still practised, other styles of writing have become important. Children may be expected to write letters of complaint, film reviews, e-mails asking for information, descriptions of the characteristics of a car or computer to be bought, newspaper articles or campaign leaflets. Teachers find that as writing skills develop, pupils are able to write in many different ways, and that their writing doesn't just copy the way they speak. How can parents help? As with reading, you can get your children to feel that writing is a normal, familiar, activity, by writing yourself, or talking about how you'd like to write. Again, they could help you, and you could encourage particular forms of writing. Get them to write postcards, when you are on holiday, and thank-you letters for presents received. Give them diaries in which to write what they think or what they are doing (and don't read the diary, unless invited, if you want them to continue), and ask them to write to complain about something they've suffered from. A child with a letter published in a local paper is a child with a sense of the excitement of writing.

When children are doing homework, parents may worry about the standard or style of their writing. If your children welcome help, you could help correct or redraft work. However, in this as in so much homework, if you just become another teacher, children may become confused or torn between 'teachers'. That's why offering help is more important then giving it. If you think that your children's work is not being corrected enough by the teacher, then you could point this out to them, and ask what they would like you to do (e.g. do it yourself, talk to the teacher). If they say 'go away', then just remember what the problem is, and offer help again when they are more receptive. You could also tell the teacher about your worries, in the homework diary or at a Parents' Evening.

Nowadays, the physical skills of writing are less important, because so much communication uses computers. Children who dislike writing may enjoy using computers, as they are 'neat' and don't look untidy when mistakes are corrected. Access to a computer can therefore raise the confidence of poor writers, and can help all writers with drafting and redrafting work. If you don't have and can't get a computer, you may have a relative who could let your children use one, and libraries, along with schools themselves, increasingly let children use computers after school and in the evenings.

- Listening.

The skill of listening is not just about 'hearing', but about how children can understand and analyse what people say, in real life as well as on the television. Helping children gain better listening skills is a complex task. Part of it is about saying things that are worth listening to: talking to children about important matters — matters that are important to you and the family, not necessarily world events — will give them a reason to listen. Showing them that you listen, too, should help: commenting on what people have said, or why you think they said it, or what they *really* meant, and so on. Listening is also about following a conversation. We've all seen television interviewers who never listen to the answers given by the guest, and we've all been in arguments where no one listens and everyone just says (or shouts) what they think, over and over. There's no great harm in any of this, as long as your children also see the opposite: good interviewers, and people having conversations in which they listen to each other.

Effective listening skills include attitude and body language. People may nod or shake their heads, or frown or smile, or say 'oh!' or 'eh?', or look at the talker. All of these actions give the impression of a good listener, just as turning away, showing no expression, or looking away may be taken as a sign of a poor listener. Parents can encourage their children to develop such skills, and can do that most easily by practising them themselves.

There are some good exercises that may help improve listening skills. The simplest, I find, is to ask someone about what has just been said: personally, I can never remember what was said on a weather forecast, even when it has just finished. Ask children (as I do, after the weather's been on) what has been said, either because you want their help, or because you enjoy the quiz. Children are also often good sources of information about plots of complicated films or series, and they can tell you what happened while you were out of the room.

● Speaking.

Speaking, like listening, seems easy to do, but can be developed to a high level, with help. Parents can encourage their children to talk about different topics (by asking them about the topics!), and can help them take different points of view, for example by saying 'yes, but what would you think if you were me?' It is important that children learn how to be flexible, and can talk in different ways for different purposes: talking to a friend, a teacher, a shopkeeper, a police officer, may all require different skills. Parents sometimes think that schools want them (and their children) to talk 'properly', or in 'Standard English'. This is not quite true, although it isn't quite false, either. The National Curriculum does aim to teach children Standard English, as this is a useful form of English. But it also promotes other forms of English. Parents do no harm to their children if they speak in non-standard forms a lot of the time. There is, though, some evidence that it helps if parents speak in Standard English some of the time. My advice is, speak in as many different ways as possible, and encourage your children to use different forms, too. In the 1960s, when more people in schools were worried about the gap between middle class and working class children, some people said that teachers thought more of middle class children because they, like their parents (and like the teachers) often used several different styles of talking, including long, complex sentences using abstract words. If your children learn how to speak in different ways, either by copying you or by copying other people, they will be at an advantage.

The description of styles of speaking sound like a lesson in acting, and drama is, indeed, part of the English syllabus. There may be few opportunities in the home for putting on a Shakespeare play, but children can still act (don't we know it!), and parents can encourage various types of acting, including, for example, making audio or video tapes for relatives in distant countries. Being allowed to 'play their part' in ceremonies or big events, such as weddings or family conferences, can also help develop skills that are useful for this area of English.

CHAPTER 21

Supporting Maths and Science skills

This is the hardest chapter of all to write, as parents have such hugely varied skills in Maths and Science, ranging from professional expertise at a higher level than most of the teachers, to blind panic at the very mention of the subjects. There's some good news and some bad news. The good news for panickers (and bad news for the talented) is that mathematical and scientific skills are probably not inherited in the genes. The bad news for panickers (and good news for the talented) is that fear, like confidence, is passed on whenever you're with your child. My first piece of advice, therefore, is try not to pass on your own fear of the subject, if you are fearful, or at least make up a convincing alibi. Try 'I'm brilliant at Maths, but I hated my Maths teacher so I intentionally failed', or 'I know everything there is to know about Chemistry, but it will be better for you if you find it all out for yourself'. A second piece of advice, also consoling the panickers, I hope, is that it will do children no good, in the long run, if parents do their homework for them. If homework were just a test of the skills of the parents, then why bother sending the children to school: why not just go yourself? There are several ways of helping your child in Maths and Science, whatever your own skills, and these are based on some of the real basics of what makes a mathematician or scientist.

- Puzzles are important.

  All school subjects involve questions, of course, but in Maths and Science, the questions are often very 'pure'. What I mean is that the questions are interesting in themselves, whether the answers are obviously useful or valuable. When we ask why Romeo fell for Juliet or why World War One started, the questions are clearly part of a larger attempt to understand Shakespeare's play or the relationship between countries: the answers are significant. When we ask what the square root is of 125, or why adding salt to water doesn't necessarily increase the volume, the question itself is interesting, however useful or useless the answer. Don't get me wrong: of course Maths and Science are useful, absolutely essential to the life of everyone. Yet a characteristic of scientists and mathematicians is that they can find questions interesting in their 'pure' form, as pure puzzles. Einstein, working on the purest of pure, apparently useless, Physics problems, came up with $E=mc^2$, and inadvertently laid the foundations for the development of nuclear bombs. Einstein is a model of a pure scientist. Your child may not be Einstein, but you can help with Maths and Science simply by encouraging solving puzzles. That includes 'game' puzzles in magazines, but also everyday puzzles. Ask them, on a journey, why they never get to the end of a rainbow, or why dogs have tails, or what makes night and day, or how much room a million Mars Bars would take up. Such joy in puzzling will help them be better, keener, mathematicians and scientists. And talking informally about the subjects will help them (and you) connect the subjects to everyday life.

- Logic.

It's not that other subjects defy the laws of logic, it's just that with Science, and even more with Maths, there's often little else. Logic is about reasoning in a step-by-step way, saying what you mean, and above all being consistent. The key rule of logic is that if something is true, it can't be false at the same time. One way of saying that is 'not (A and not-A)' or 'you can't have your cake and eat it'. Being logical with your child, and helping him or her be logical, can benefit Maths and Science. It is worth pointing out that the laws of logic are spectacularly obvious, until you try bringing up children: arguing with your children tests the limits of logic in ways philosophers wouldn't dare. Children may not want to go out, but may not want to stay at home either. They may not want any of the food on offer, or any other food in the world, but may also not want to miss the meal. A birthday party is the worst idea in the world, but not having a party is also the worst idea in the world. Are they being intentionally illogical? My own interpretation of most of these contradictions is that they are signs of unhappiness. 'I don't want to go out and I don't want not to go out' really means 'I'm unhappy, if I go out I'll still be unhappy and I don't want this, if I don't go out I'll still be unhappy and I don't want this'. 'I don't want food and I don't want to have no food' might mean 'I want to be dead, and then I won't have to worry about food'. Although sad, the second versions are at least logical. Parents can help their children be more logical, by gently getting underneath the apparent contradictions: children may get away with being grumpy and unhappy, but there's no need for them to get away with being illogical! And parents can also help by being consistent and logical themselves. So 'smoking is bad for you' whilst unapologetically smoking, is less logical than saying 'smoking is bad for you, I wish I'd never started, so I hope you don't get trapped like me'. (Teachers are the same: they happily rush off for a cigarette after teaching a lesson on the dangers of smoking.) The logical way of approaching the topic is likely to be more effective, and, the point of this run through logic, it is likely to help children with their studies, especially with Maths and Science. Some people (starting with Socrates) even say that everyone already knows all the answers to mathematical problems, and all it takes to get to the answer is a guide to get the person to take one logical step at a time. I'm not so sure that Socrates was right here, but logic certainly takes you a long way. It's what experienced teachers who don't want to appear ignorant often do when pupils ask them difficult questions: 'Now let's see, what would be a good starting point ...'.

- Workings.

Teachers are often more concerned about how the problem was worked out than whether or not the answer was right. Many parents complain that the teacher is unfair, because their child was given a low grade despite having got the answer right: a situation often spiced-up by the fact that it was the parent who worked out the answer, so the parent felt personally insulted by the grade. Workings, whether we like it or not, are vital to Maths and Science. Myself, I like workings. When a plumber comes round to fix the central heating, or I visit the doctor, I like to know exactly how they come to their diagnosis. What are the symptoms of a failed thermocouple or an arthritic joint? By knowing how they came to their conclusions, I can have more or, usually, less confidence in their skill. I'll also know, next time, what to do, and will be more likely to know whether the treatment given was effective because of a lucky fluke or because of the plumber's/doctor's skill and understanding. I have little trust in the plumber or doctor who says 'I don't know, I'll just have to replace the boiler' or 'I don't know, but you might as well try these antibiotics'. The same goes for pupils who don't show their workings. The two good things about this, for parents, is that you don't need to worry so much about the answer, and that, whatever your skill, you can always 'guide' your child through the workings, saying 'explain why you did that; now, write all that down'.

Maths

A brief description of National Curriculum Maths may help you to understand the work, and reports on your children's work, a little better. The first thing to say is that Maths skills should be used. The use or application of Maths, in solving real problems, is what gives Maths its hook on reality, and what gives parents plenty of opportunities to 'use' the skills of their children. From simple activities, like checking change given in shops, to more complex calculations, like comparing the prices of drinks in different sized bottles, parents can ask their children for advice, and children, if they give advice, will be practising and learning more Maths. There are so many chances to do this, on journeys and holidays, or at home, whilst decorating a room or paying bills. Parents who are confident mathematicians can set and check interesting challenges, parents with less confidence can be honestly in their children's debt. And if you win the lottery, they can always work out how you could spend the money!

Number work includes what most people think of as 'real' Maths, arithmetic (including multiplication tables), but I like to think of numbers as having special, almost magical, properties. The sort of investigative work that children do in Maths these days, tries to get them to understand how numbers work, and what properties they have. When I lived in a house whose number was 210, I was told that 210 was the sum of all the numbers from 1 to 20, and I've never forgotten. Children studying Maths are likely to have that sort of feeling for numbers. It is difficult knowing how parents can help children gain that sense of wonder, if they don't have it themselves. Perhaps the best advice is to say 'that *is* interesting' to children who make interesting number discoveries.

Algebra, where numbers are replaced by letters or symbols (including graphs), where Maths becomes more abstract, is sometimes a bit of a shock for pupils. They have just got used to working with numbers, and the numbers disappear. It's like taking the stabilisers off a child's bike: some children will quickly learn how to ride without them, others will fall off and never want to get back on. Parents can help with algebra by getting their children to go over the problems very carefully, in their own time, as algebraic questions often have quite a simple solution built in to them. Slow, careful, safe work on these problems, if they are found difficult, will help just as slow, careful, cycling without stabilisers.

Shape, space and measurement come next. This is a 'seeing' area of Maths, with skills related to skills in Art, and help can be offered in many forms. Decorative patterns, dividing food, making models, or tiling a garden path can all help and encourage children to understand this topic. Finally, pupils are expected to be able to handle data, putting together information into tables and graphs, and interpreting other people's tables and graphs. Included in this is dealing with averages and probabilities. As with some of the basic arithmetical problems, parents can actually use a lot of the skills of their children, here. Not just (please) working out the chances of winning the lottery, but also doing data logging and interpretation — when sorting out provisions for a big wedding, or working out insurance policies, or getting to grips with what political parties say they have done or will do for us.

If you are checking homework, rather than asking for help with real-life problems, then it is worth noting that there are likely to be particular techniques or methods that the teacher will want your children to use. Again, your children will be the experts on this, and an offer of help is better than insistent correction.

Science

The Science National Curriculum has been changed several times, to make it simpler and more like older more traditional versions of Science. An important principle of Science in school is that pupils should investigate and experiment: they should actually *be* scientists, not just learn *about* Science. Helping children at home can mean getting them to think about how they would find out about or solve a problem. Trying things out would be useful, too, though I can understand that parents will be a little wary of 'experiments'. In schools, children will be scientific about 'life processes and living things' (which is a long name for Biology), 'materials and their properties' (Chemistry), and 'physical processes' (Physics). Each of these areas, in their own ways, are full of 'wonder' – the mystery of how the human body works, the shock of chemical changes, or the awful simplicity of the Solar System. Children can discover some of this through books and, increasingly, exciting CD-Roms. They can also be encouraged simply to look around them.

CHAPTER 22

Supporting History, Geography, Religious Education, and Modern Foreign Languages

Four big subjects, all very different and all important in their own ways. What links them is people, so they are sometimes referred to as Humanities. They are all concerned with how people think, behave and deal with each other and with their environments. Modern Foreign Languages (MFL, or, for most pupils, French, German or Spanish) looks at how people communicate, just as English does, but more than this, it should investigate the culture or life of people in countries speaking those languages. That takes it closer to Geography and the other 'people' subjects. There are therefore some ways in which you can help your child in all of the subjects at once.

● People.
In all these subjects, pupils learn about people, including themselves and people like themselves, and people who are very different. It helps their studies if they can understand other people, and see things from their point of view. Tolerance of different people and openness to their views, are required (if not always practised) by every school, and are built in to various parts of the National Curriculum. They are valuable qualities in themselves, but they are also academically useful. Parents can help their children by encouraging tolerance and openness. It is important to be clear about how controversial this may be, and to leave the choice up to parents. Tolerance includes tolerance of people whose views you may find repugnant: children may be asked to write about what it would be like to be a Nazi stormtrooper, or why some atheists believe that talk of gods is nonsensical. Tolerance doesn't mean giving up any sense of right and wrong, or giving up campaigning to promote your views or attack other views or behaviour. But it does, in this context, mean being able to find out about different views in an open atmosphere, so that if, in the end, your children decide to agree or disagree with a particular set of beliefs, they will have done so for good reasons, and not just out of habit or prejudice. Schools are not being

completely neutral in this: they will (they have to) say that racist behaviour is unacceptable in school, but they will also try to help pupils understand why people may be racist. The same can be said of parents: promote whatever views you want, but your children will be better able to study the Humanities if they feel able to think about and explore all kinds of different views.

- Places.

Wherever you are with your child, in your own neighbourhood, travelling on holiday or moving home, be curious about places. Think about, or get your child to think about, why the place is the way it is, how it has changed, and how it might change in the future. What sort of people live there, and what do they do? How does it compare with other places? Are there any 'special' places in the area — places with special personal, historical or religious significance? What makes them special? Why are places the shape they are? Most towns follow the shape and pattern of rivers, fields, hills and marshes that pre-dated them, and have unique characteristics, ways of living and making money, accents and languages, faith communities, transport networks and connections with other places. Places may, for a time, be dominated by natural or human disasters (Kobe, Pompeii, Chernobyl), historic events (Battle near Hastings, Jerusalem), physical features (the Himalayas, the Everglades), or much else. Parents can encourage curiosity in their children, and this will hugely benefit learning in the Humanities.

- Investigation.

The Humanities, like Science, often include investigative work. Humanities investigations may at times be less systematic than in Science, but they are just as important. There will be questions to ask people and things to look up in books, and there will be objects and places to investigate. Having books, especially encyclopaedias, or the equivalent on the computer, and having plenty of trips to museums and places or countries of interest, will all benefit such investigative work. All can be expensive, though, and the good news for the hard-up is that the key to investigative work is people and curiosity, and making good use of any resources that are available. I'm told that computer programmers in Russia are often more imaginative than those in the UK or USA, because they can't afford such expensive computers and ready-made programmes. If you have got the money to support investigative work with books, computers and trips, then that's great. Ask the school for advice on what to get or where to go, to be on the safe side. If you haven't got the money, then go for quality, not quantity, and your child should do just as well.

- Meaning.

What makes people different to other animals, as far as we know, is that they give *meaning* to the world around them. A mirror is just something to look at and peck, for a budgerigar, but to people it can be a sign of vanity, a source of bad luck, or an entrance to Alice's looking-glass house. A cross can have a religious meaning; the shape of a landscape can mean, to a geographer, that glaciers were once here. The whole French language is, of course, a system of meanings. The year 1789 can mean something to an historian, and even more to a French person, historian or not. To help your child in these subjects, the question 'what does this mean?' is therefore a good starting point. Some things mean a lot to people, perhaps their religious or political views, or their country, or their enemies. Children can therefore be helped, too, to understand that 'meaning' isn't just about words and symbols, but about passions, loyalties, and, well, the meaning of life!

History

History is one of the more straightforward parts of the National Curriculum. The topics to be taught are clearly set out, with little room for manoeuvre, and there are plenty of ways in which parents can help their children very directly, for example by taking children to visit a castle. The periods that must be taught in Key Stage 3 (between the ages of 11 and 14) are Medieval Britain (starting with the Battle of Hastings in 1066 and ending in 1500), the Making of the United Kingdom (Britain from 1500 to 1750), Britain in the Industrial Revolution (from 1750 to 1900), and the 20th Century World (including the two world wars). Pupils must also study one other topic in European History (most popular are the Roman Empire, or the French Revolution), and one past non-European society (most popular are Islamic civilisations, or the indigenous peoples of North America, or black people of the Americas). Because there are only a few variations, and all the topics have to be taught in roughly the same order (starting with the earliest and ending with the 20th century), there are plenty of books on each topic, and most have been written for the 'right' age of pupils. There are also plenty of places to visit, especially as so much of the syllabus is about Britain. Some enterprising person will presumably organise tours, tied in to the National Curriculum, where all you need to do is tell the tour company the ages of your children, and they will arrange the rest.

There's more to History than a list of topics, of course. Children need to understand how History moves from one period to the next, and how events and periods fit together. They must look at different interpretations of the same event, and they must look at real sources of evidence for what happened and why. They also have to be able to describe what they have found out. A sense of time passing, then, must be matched by empathy with and understanding of different people, investigative skills, and the ability to communicate effectively. The hardest thing for parents to do, in my experience, is to be comfortable with the fact that there are few certainties in History. One person's hero is another's villain, and one country's crusade is another country's invasion. People are used to a fair bit of uncertainty in real life, and everyone knows that, whatever your views on politics or religion, there will be plenty of people who disagree with you. Some, however, look to History as a source of certainty, like they look to doctors for definitive treatments: certainty about their origins or their place in the world, and certain justifications for what they and their country have done in the past. The National Curriculum, like the National Health Service, doesn't offer certainty. Historians, like doctors, will have a good rummage around, and will do the best they can, but a second or third opinion can always come up with something different.

The joys of History, for parents and children, are mostly the joys of stories, the joys of experiences and visits, and the joys of finding out from mysterious clues. It is a subject that retains the excitement of Primary school, for most pupils, and parents can join with this pleasure.

Geography

Like History, Geography at Key Stage 3 has quite a limited number of topics to be investigated, so parents can be well prepared. The places to be studied in depth are the UK plus two of Australia/New Zealand, Europe, Japan, North America, Russia, Asia (excluding Japan), South and Central America and the Caribbean. Parents may want to get their children maps or globes, and could follow events in the countries being studied (having found out which they are from the school) by cutting out articles from newspapers or magazines and following events on the television. A few Geography teachers were appalled with themselves, for example, when they found themselves 'pleased' (for their teaching) that there was a large earthquake in Japan.

Once the countries have been chosen, there is a set of themes to be investigated using as many Geographical skills as possible: tectonic processes (such as earthquakes volcanoes), geomorphological processes (the shape of the land, coasts, floods and so on), weather and climate (including how they 'work', and what effects they have), ecosystems (such as tropical rain forests), population (including why people move), settlement (about towns and villages, and what places to live are like), economics (looking at industry, in particular), development (the ways in which societies change, and how they are connected to each other), and the environment (including water, energy, pollution, and much more). Once parents know that these are the types of issues that can come up in Geography — that it is a very broad subject — they can be better prepared to support homework. The best way of encouraging Geographical skills, though, is not to learn all about all the topics, but to ask the right sort of questions. The questions, set out in the National Curriculum, may seem obvious, but can be used in many different contexts. What and where is a place? What is it like? How did it get like this, and how and why is it changing? What are the implications or effects of these changes?

Religious Education

Of all the subjects that must be taught in schools, Religious Education (RE) is the one that is not described in the National Curriculum. Instead, each area works out its own syllabus, with the Government just giving models of good practice. (The whole of schooling works like this in Scotland.) In fact, much RE is quite similar throughout the country. Nearly all schools teach six major world religions in depth — Christianity, Buddhism, Hinduism, Islam, Judaism, and Sikhism — and they either look at each religion in turn, or look at themes (such as birth and death, or celebrations, or gods), with each theme addressed by all the religions. Many schools will include a lot of general moral issues and dilemmas with RE, and when this is done, the beliefs of 'non-believers' often take a bigger rôle than in courses studying the religions quite separately.

When it comes to parental support, I have pointed out the most important issues in the general introduction to this chapter. I would simply add the 'all or nothing' nature of the subject. Parents can't pick and choose which religions their children should study, although they can withdraw their children altogether from RE. If parents allow their children to study religions, it would be most helpful to help children be open to understanding all the religions and the cultures associated with them.

Openness is not the same as giving up beliefs or faith, which should, I would hope, be able to be maintained while trying to understand different beliefs. Religious Education is quite different, in this way, from the official version of Assemblies, in which children are expected to worship, and mostly worship within the Christian tradition. (I say the 'official version', because so many school refuse to follow the regulations.)

Modern Foreign Languages

Modern Foreign Languages teaching is similar to English teaching, not surprisingly, with skills being developed in reading, writing, listening and speaking. To simplify the curriculum further, the National Curriculum says what topics are to be covered, and these are everyday activities (the language of classroom, home and school, including food, health and fitness); personal and social life (self, family, social activities, holidays and special occasions); and the world around us (home town and area, the natural and the made environment, and people, places and customs). In Key Stage 4 (between 14 and 16), these topics are added to, with the world of work (further education and training, careers, and the language of the workplace); and the international world (tourism, and world events and issues).

Parents can support this work in various ways, the most obvious being trips to countries speaking the language, or exchanges between your children and children who live there, or setting up pen-pal or Internet correspondences. Language learning tapes and CD-Roms are easily available, and people with cable or satellite television can generally access foreign language programmes. Parents could also be prepared to be taught the language by their children — as they will learn more if they are teaching someone. Many children, though, find languages a bit embarrassing, so don't be too surprised if they don't ask for much help, or if you don't hear them chatting away in their newly-learnt language. That's the great advantage of tapes and CD Roms. The best time to learn a foreign language is probably during Primary school years. Not many Primary schools teach MFL, and the National Curriculum only makes it compulsory in Secondary school. Nevertheless, parents who really want to help their children with MFL could best give help in those early years, when brains seem to be spongier and levels of embarrassment lower.

CHAPTER 23

Supporting the Arts, Technical and Physical skills

Much learning can be passive, and is about absorbing and communicating information or ideas. These, however, are the 'doing' subjects: intellectual too, but distinctive for how they are creative and physically involving. This characteristic leads to the first piece of advice: supporting these subjects means helping and encouraging your child to be active. A young child will be taken to the park, pushed on swings, encouraged to draw and paint, and allowed to shove square pegs in square holes. Eventually the bright little pictures will be taken off the fridge, and the toy xylophone given to jumble. Some of the principles, however, can stay with you forever.

● Young children often seem unself-conscious, painting freely (not doing pictures 'by the rules'), making up dances and songs, literally throwing themselves into their games. As they grow older, they respond more to criticism and become more sensitive to other people's views of them. The susceptibility of teenage children to praise and criticism can dominate their artistic, technical and physical activities: their lives sometimes seem to be driven by nothing but embarrassment. Supporting these subjects is a delicate matter for parents. Allow them to keep their paintings or piano playing to themselves, rather than forcing them into the public (even if you did pay for the paints or the lessons): the odd word of praise may have to substitute for the fridge gallery. Praise physical accomplishments, but not to such an extent that you've got nothing left to praise if growing up means unavoidable, or even avoidable, physical changes. Mending a bike or cooking a meal may make a bit of a mess, but it can also help develop important skills. (Clearing up helps develop important skills too, of course.) Technical skills are often learnt simply by looking on, and this is another reason why your child doing their homework in the kitchen, while you cook, may be positively useful.

- Equipment may help with these subjects, with workshops, studios, rehearsal areas, or multi-gyms all very exciting. Improvisation, however, is and has always been more important. A cardboard box can be a boat, to an artistic child, a dead cow can be a work of art; a table-top can be a drum set, and a flight of stairs can provide enough steps for an exercise routine. Where you do feel under pressure to get equipment to support your child's education, I'd recommend adaptable and reusable equipment over specialised and single-purpose equipment. So a workbench rather than a mini-kiln, an electronic keyboard rather than a bass clarinet. In fact, I'd be cruel enough to say that a good rule for spending money on equipment for your children is that you'd like to use it yourself. Then, if they get bored, you have something useful.
- With young children, it is easy to see their delight in their achievements, in skills that we take for granted, like being able to walk. Older children, though, are also constantly discovering things we may take for granted, and parents can encourage them in this. Mending a puncture, decorating a bedroom, making scrambled eggs on toast, or doing a high jump, may all be most exciting because of their novelty, and the pleasure in such achievements should be celebrated.

Art

Art is more than Art in the National Curriculum, as it includes crafts and design. This is particularly important when dealing with the 'knowledge and understanding' bits of the subject. Pupils are expected to find out about the works of people in the past and from different countries. Many parents assume this is all about 'great artists', and think that they will have to get expensive books of prints of great paintings. Certainly, such books will be useful and fascinating, and have become unaccountably cheap in recent years, but getting to know the works of artists, in this sense, includes the teapot on the kitchen table, and the table, and, in fact, the whole house. Parents are helping their children with this subject, then, simply by having designed objects all around them, with further help coming from talking about the qualities these objects have. So, if a parent is uncertain about the aesthetic qualities of a painting by Vermeer, no need to worry: discuss the buildings in the street, and the objects you've chosen in your home and why you chose them. This is real homework: work on your home!

Getting children to understand paintings is important too, of course. Curiosity, and a willingness to go into the odd gallery (or give your child the bus fare, at least), are the most useful qualities here. My favourite 'gallery' task, also recommended in Chapter 10, is to get children to choose their three favourite paintings, and say why they have chosen them. A simple and stress-free task.

The other half of Art is 'making'. As with Design and Technology, the product can't just appear out of thin air. Pupils must investigate: they must observe. This preparatory side of 'making' (as opposed to painting, for example) seems to me to be the biggest section of Art work that parents underestimate or ignore. Close observation, and the recording of detail, is more like Science than Art, some might say, and there are indeed links. Pupils should think scientifically in Art, as it is out of a detailed investigation into patterns, textures, shapes, colours and forms, that Art can develop with confidence. It would be difficult to understand how anyone could hope to create a beautiful object who could see no beauty in the natural and made world. So parents can help with this side of Art by encouraging careful observation: rather as careful listening is a help with English skills.

Music

Music is divided into performance and theory. Parents sometimes think that the subject is all about theory and listening, as it was for many pupils in the past. But performance is in there, and can be supported by parents in many ways, including listening. Listening to children perform, if they allow this, can make it all worthwhile, for you and them, but listening is a skill of the performer too. Performers who can listen to themselves will be able to improve. Listening in English, listening in MFL, looking in Art, listening in Music: these are skills developed by imitation, and requiring no great knowledge. All parents can help, and in Music and Art, they should find it very easy to enjoy helping.

Pupils have to analyse music of many different styles and from many different countries. Skills of analysis are really skills of description. Key words include pitch (how high or low a note is), duration (how long it lasts), dynamics (how loud or soft it gets), tempo (how fast or slow), timbre (the quality of the sound, like the difference between a guitar note and a note on a flute), and texture (the mixture of sounds). Along with these sorts of descriptions, pupils should analyse the structure of a piece of music. Most music depends on repetition: verse, chorus, verse, for example. Parents can help, as with Geography, simply by asking these kinds of questions. There is music nearly all around us, and pupils can improve their skills in analysis by answering these questions about any piece of music, so just keep asking!

Design and Technology

Design and Technology includes, unsurprisingly, designing things (design) and making them (technology). There is a single approach to what used to be several subjects: craft (making things in wood, metal, plastic, and also making electronic products), textiles, and food. Pupils or parents who forget the links are likely to miss out on the qualities of the subject that can best be supported at home. Some 'making' can be done at home, especially when it comes to food, where there is no need to get specialist equipment, but it is the design stage that homes are best equipped for. Design doesn't just mean doing a drawing or written description of the product to be made. It includes looking at similar products already made, thinking about alternative designs, planning materials, and so on. Parents and children can discuss these issues, building up ideas based on knowledge of products in the home, perhaps, and the dialogue can continue with 'evaluative' work, looking at preferences and choices of products. As well as investigating products themselves, and their materials and structures, pupils must investigate the quality of products. Design and Technology promote the 'demanding customer', and any parent going in to a shop with a child fresh out of a Design and Technology lesson should get a full evaluation of the products on offer. Alternatively, if the parents are already 'demanding customers', then their children should do well in Design and Technology.

Information Technology

Information Technology (IT) means computers, to most people, including most teachers. The simplest way of supporting IT outside school is to give children access to a computer — either at home or in a local library or homework centre, or in the home of a friendly relative. It certainly shouldn't be necessary to have such access, but it will still be helpful. The type of computer to get, if you are getting one for the home, will depend on how much money is available, now and in the future — the spending doesn't stop when you get a computer home, but must be spent on getting information, for example on CDs or on the Internet (using the phone line). If I were to recommend a computer here, my advice would be out of date by the time the book hit the bookshelves. Just shop around, and buy lots of magazines before you start looking more closely.

IT can be supported at home, though, without any computer. If parents are aware of the possible uses of computers, and their problems, they can talk about this with their children, and if they are not so sure, they can ask their children. Children will also benefit from 'touch typing' skills (i.e. typing without looking at the keyboard), and this can be practised on an old typewriter or a cheap word processor or, at a push, on a piece of paper.

Physical Education (PE)

PE is rather more than sport, so unsporting parents shouldn't feel left out. The aim of PE in the National Curriculum is to help children be physically active, healthy, and with good posture, understanding and practising fair play, and coping with success and limitations. It is an all-round education, then, promoting a long and healthy life, not just beating people. Many are surprised to discover how much of PE could actually be done whilst sitting in front of the television: reviewing matches, analysing rules, looking into how 'fairly' people compete, and so on. A critical viewing, then, as I recommended for English, can help your child with PE. Of course, the active side of PE is the most important one. There are three strategies for supporting active PE at home.

- Exercise can be promoted for its own sake — for pleasure — and children have a huge range of activities that are popular and easily, and often cheaply, available. Some children prefer team games or group activities like aerobics classes, others prefer more isolated pursuits like jogging. The exercise is likely to be effective in the long term only if the child has chosen it. There are many things that are good for us that we ignore. Children may like to know that some exercise can be done at the same time as other activities: an exercise bike goes well with reading or television.

- Exercise can be promoted more sneakily, as a by-product of another activity. Until only a few years ago, most children walked to school, now few do. The same happened to shopping. What is left? Walking the dog and going to dances are probably good examples of by-product exercise, with gardening and decorating providing good exercise but unpopular with many children. Parents could presumably think of more examples suited to their circumstances.

- Health can be promoted in many ways — healthy diet, healthy posture, a reasonable amount of sleep, regular check-ups at the doctors, and avoiding damaging and addictive (and expensive) drugs like tobacco or heroin. A fine list, this, and all covered by the PE curriculum and the cross-curricular theme of health. But how can parents actually get their children to do all of these things? Partly by example (living healthy lives yourselves), partly by providing opportunities (for example, having healthy food in the house, and having chairs that support backs), partly by informing children (either from your own knowledge or from information in libraries or schools), partly by helping your child be happy enough to avoid a downward spiral of self-destructive or unhealthy behaviour. Easy, eh? Good luck.

CHAPTER 24

Coursework and examinations

'Project' 'coursework' and 'dissertation' are three words for the same thing, done at different ages: an extended piece of work, studied in depth and unique to the person doing it. Coursework is mostly done outside formal lessons: a lot is done entirely at home. Since the mid-1980s, projects have become one of the favourite homework tasks for Primary school, as they had to do lessons in more and more subjects, and could no longer spend all day on projects in the classroom. At the same time, GCSEs were introduced, since when, coursework has meant grades. Exams have always meant grades, of course, and it is the special qualities of GCSE coursework and' exams, and how to help your child get better grades, that I want to address here. (Success in earlier exams, such as SATs, may also benefit, but I've focused here on GCSEs, which are the the most important exams for nearly all pupils.) GCSEs come at a difficult age, when children are, in general, least welcoming of parental involvement. That's not your fault, or theirs — a lot of it is down to Biology. For many parents, staying out of the way will be the 'help' most asked for. Yet parents can help, at times, and for these rare moments, here goes. For the rest of the time, just remember what a good job you did getting them in to adolescence, and remember that it will eventually end.

Coursework

- The assessment of coursework gives more credit for obedience and hard work than for flair or intelligence. You can help children more by helping them work hard, over the whole period of the course, and reading the instructions carefully, when it comes to coursework, than you can by giving them 'answers' or interesting ideas.
- Coursework is stressful but it belongs to children, not parents: if parents are so much in charge of the coursework that the children no longer feel it belongs to them, then they will end up stressed and out of control, which means doubly stressed.

- Coursework will benefit from research, but it is not all about libraries or finding piles of books. The *use* made of research is more important. It is certainly comforting to copy out a barrel-load of information, but after the first few pages, few extra marks will be gained.
- Completed coursework will benefit by looking good, and parents can help with this, but three days on a front cover won't get as many marks as three days on a new chapter or section. Similarly, around 5% of the marks will be given for correct spelling, punctuation and grammar, and parents can often help with this, but, again, most of the marks will still come from other qualities.
- Evaluation. Pupils have to know, for most subjects, what went wrong and what else could have been done. This goes against the grain, and sometimes feels a little artificial or grudging, as if we would say to Mr Daimler 'Okay, so you've made a petrol-engined car, but what other systems of transport could you have designed?' Nevertheless, good evaluation can and should be the basis of further study. ('So, what next, Mr Daimler?' seems reasonable enough.) Evaluation also gets more marks, and is often what makes the difference between grades C and B or A. Being self-critical, as evaluation sections often requires pupils to be, can hurt, and so is often better done by pupils with plenty of self-confidence. If your child refuses to admit that anything in his or her coursework could possibly be improved, this is probably a sign of low self-confidence. For those pupils, I try to make sure I use the word 'and', not 'but'. 'That's a great design, and it could also be the basis of another, modified, six wheel design', sounds better than 'That's a great design, but haven't you thought of trying a modified, six wheel design?' In the same way, 'This shopping survey looks useful, and I'm sure it could also have been used in a market or out-of-town mall' sounds better than 'This shopping survey looks useful, but didn't you think of surveying a market or out-of-town mall?' By using 'and' instead of 'but', you and your child can see evaluation as a positive thing and not as altogether negative criticism.

Examinations

- If you worry about your child's exams, worry, earlier, about the courses. The best way to help with exams is to help with the courses. Don't think of exams as completely separate from courses, to be worried about for years in advance: your child is likely to be even more fearful of them, and may ignore the obvious technique of working hard throughout the two years.
- An exam tests many skills, and not just those of the 'subject' being examined. Exams test language skills, planning, concentration, timing,

and temperament. Parents can help children with these skills, even if they know nothing about Geography or Food Technology or Sociology. Pupils will benefit if they are used to reading and following instructions, have planned their revision, can concentrate for an hour or three, can time what they do and balance the time spent on different tasks, and keep reasonably cool under pressure. They can learn these skills by example — if you have these qualities, they should be able to copy you. They can also learn them despite example — if you don't have these skills, but panic and give up at the first obstacle, they may learn to avoid this, especially if you can say 'I always give up on difficult tasks; I'm so proud of your ability to keep going and work through your difficulties'.

- Opticians, when they test your eyes, will say of each lens 'better, worse, or just the same'. They don't expect to come up with perfect lenses first time, but just work to improve a little on the previous lens. The same approach can be helpful for exams. Whatever has been done before, your children can still do something to improve their exam results — a small improvement, perhaps, but an improvement. No revision and it's May already? Well, a couple of weeks of revision will make the result better; a couple of weeks of couch potatoing will make them worse. No revision and there's an exam tomorrow? Even a day's revision can only make things better. It is easier to think of a little piece of work as being a little helpful, than to ponder over the mass of work that might be needed to get the perfect result. Parents can help, by suggesting such incremental improvements, rather than only talking about the massive amount of work needed for perfection.

- A book written by John Holt in the 1960s was called *How Children Fail* and it looked at young children and how scared they were in the classroom. They were scared to give the wrong answer when a teacher asked a question, so they gave no answer at all. Failure, then, is often an intentional 'action', and is not simply about ignorance or stupidity. I've never yet come across a pupil who wants to do badly in exams. However, I've known many who have done badly partly or entirely because they didn't revise properly. Pupils respond differently to pressure: the most common response is to give up, or to fail intentionally. That's why the common parental pleas 'But don't you know how important your GCSEs are?', and 'Don't you want to do well?', are worthy but generally misplaced. Yes, your children do know how important GCSEs are, and yes, they do want to do well. It's fear, fear of failure, or fear of trying hard and still failing, that makes many children fail. What can parents do to help? I wish I could say that all it needs is some quick fix, but it's a complex issue. I've worked with pupils who are at the extreme, completely unable to do any work, perhaps wanting to give up school and walk out of the exams. When talking to them, and their families, I sometimes find that pupils thought their parents only really loved them because they were clever. My advice may be a cliché, and may sound like the script of an Australian soap opera, but it still seemed to help in some of these extreme cases: Tell, convince, your children that you love them for themselves, and that, much as you'd like them to do well, you'll love them just as much whether they pass or fail, and that you are proud of who they are as well as what they've done. As I say, this seemed to help some, very troubled, pupils, and it may not work with everyone. It certainly won't work if it is done insincerely. But, other than if insincere, at least it can't do any harm.

CHAPTER 25

Communicating with the school

Homework is the key link between school and parents. Some parents may have enough knowledge or skill to teach their children at home. Most, however, will work with the school, and the best way of helping a pupil learn is for the school and family to work together. Communication is what makes this possible. Occasionally, teachers don't seem to bother about homework; occasionally, parents don't seem to bother about their children's homework; much more often, children play one off against the other, and get away with it because the school and parents don't talk. Deep down, of course, everyone wants success. So, although it may sometimes feel like a battle, parents, children and schools have a lot of aims in common, and good communication can highlight these common aims, and overcome a lot of the possible conflicts. Schools have the main responsibility for creating effective systems of communication, but this chapter is intended to help parents make good use of these systems.

Homework diaries

Homework diaries are the most common way of communicating. As a teacher, I certainly don't expect all the parents of my pupils to know all about History, Science, or whatever, or to spend every spare moment helping their children with their homework. What I most want is for parents, all of whom are interested in their children's progress, to let me know about how they think their children are doing. Where homework diaries are used, I'll get the pupils to write the homework in the diary. If the children go home and parents don't see any homework in the diary, they should either worry about the children ('did you forget to write the homework in your diary?') or worry about the teachers ('did they not set you any homework?'). In both cases, it would help the teachers if you wrote in the diary 'Please remind Zoe to put her homework in the diary' or 'I'm worried that Zoe isn't being given much homework these days'.

The most common complaint about homework, from parents, is that there is not enough, and the complaints come up most often at Parents Evenings. However, it is best to give teachers, or the school, reminders as they go through the year, if you are worried about this, by commenting in a homework diary. Then, teachers can either adjust the amount of homework they give, or justify keeping the homework the same, or explain why the homework should take longer than your child spends on it. homework diaries may also be good places to write comments like 'it is difficult to do this research on a Wednesday evening, when the libraries are shut, as we don't have the right books at home'. If such reminders or suggestions are not followed up, or if there are no homework diaries, you could always arrange to visit the school or talk to the tutor or head of year.

Profiles and reports

Profiles or reports are the description by the school of what your child has done in every subject, and they should come out at least once a year. They should provide enough information for you to know how you can help your child improve. These days, most are written in a way that avoids negative comments, but lists the good qualities shown, and sets targets for future improvement. Interpreting these profiles is quite a skill. On the 'comments' section, you need to spot what *isn't* there. This book should help, as I've listed some of the skills or topics that may be covered. The 'targets' should be specific rather than vague (so 'do half an hour's reading every week' is better than 'read more'), and should be achievable before the next profile (so 'practise the perfect tense' is better than 'become fluent in French'). The profiles might say something about homework as a separate activity, although some teachers prefer looking at skills and knowledge rather than class and homework, so don't worry if homework isn't named. Certainly, they should say things that will help you support your child's homework. In the 'targets' section, there may be recommendations about behaviour or attitude in class, but there are also likely to be learning targets that could be practised at home. For most subjects, around a fifth of the work should be done at home, so any weakness could be addressed at home, even if classwork will be more important. I'd recommend talking to your children, after you get their profiles, about whether there are any ways in which you and the rest of the family can help them achieve their targets. Targets look forward, and are therefore more positive than just asking children why they didn't do better. If the profiles don't give any idea about what extra could be done, then it should be worth talking to the school.

Parents Evenings

Most Parents Evenings happen soon after profiles are produced, although there may also be some held at the start of courses, to let you know what to expect. The profile-based evenings can be more worrying for parents than teachers: parents often feel as though they are being judged, although teachers, in fact, are usually just wanting to pass on or get information about pupils. The evenings can be made more useful if parents have specific questions to ask. Most obviously, 'how can I help my child improve in this subject?'. Other questions could be about what exactly the profile means, or how the course will progress next year. The question that teachers could sensibly ask you, and you could give the answer whether or not they ask, is 'how do *you* think your child is doing in this subject?' A teacher may have 200 pupils, and can easily fail to spot anxieties, overwork, or enthusiasm about a subject. If a parent tells the teachers that a child is worried, or is really keen, it can transform their view of the child. Children are good at hiding their feelings at times, and the more you can tell teachers about feelings that would help the teachers teach more effectively, the better. I'm not recommending telling teachers what your child thinks about their dress sense, tempting as that may be, but passing on your perspective on their work. Remember that teachers are only human, and passing on good news is likely to help increase enthusiasm all round.

Work out, with your child and with the teachers, what and how improvements can be made: this should be the basis of nearly all communication between parents and schools. If homework diaries, profiles, and Parents Evenings don't achieve this, you may want to communicate in other ways. Phone calls are quick, but teachers find it difficult taking phone calls during a teaching day; letters are harder to produce, but can be answered with more care. However you communicate with the school, I'd recommend you do it after you've talked to your child, and that the communication says clearly what your impression is of your child's progress, and what you think may help, rather than (or as well as) being a more general comment on the school as a whole.

CHAPTER 26

Making the most of leisure time

I've said several times in this book, that parents can help their children with homework without having to put them under enormous stress all the time. There are restrictions on homework in many countries — it may be banned at weekends (in Denmark), or banned altogether (in Spain). The UK, apparently enjoying stress and limitless tasks, expects all schools to have homework policies and to set homework regularly, but with no upper limit. Like parenting, educating never ends. Parents needn't get caught up in this difficult situation: they generally dislike 'nagging' their children as much as the children dislike being 'nagged'. However, this chapter is about making good, educational, use of leisure time, and some may accuse me of being a spoil-sport. Perhaps I am, but I'd like to think that leisure is educational anyway, and that, by subtly guiding children to benefit more from their leisure pursuits, parents could even reduce the number of times their children say 'I'm bored'.

Holidays

Don't let schools decide your holidays for you, but if you've got choices, the school curriculum may help you decide one way or the other. For example, of the more popular attractions in South East England, Hampton Court might best be visited when your child is around 11, and the Science Museum when your child is 12 or 13, as the History topic related to Henry VIII is most often covered at the end of Year 7 or start of Year 8, and the Industrial Revolution is most often covered at the end of Year 8 or start of Year 9. If going abroad, and choosing between Greece and Rome, it may be worth knowing that Ancient Greek History is likely to be studied in Primary school, whilst Ancient Roman History is likely to be studied at the start of Secondary school. You could ask the school what topics are being covered in History, what regions or countries are being covered by Geography, what foreign languages are being offered as options in later years, or whether the Art teachers can recommend any good galleries to visit wherever you're going.

I've produced 'holiday' homework tasks for some of my pupils. Most often, I'll set these homework tasks for pupils who have holidays during term time, so that they can report back on their travels in an informative way. You may wish to use these ideas during any holiday. Here is guidance for pupils on Geography, History and RE projects, all suited to holiday work.

Geography holiday project

If you are going to be out of school for a while, you will want to get on with some work while you are away. You may be away on holiday, or visiting family in a different country, or your family may be working away from home. Your absence from school can be a great opportunity to do some good Geography work. This will be useful for you, and it will help other pupils in your class too, when you come back.

The journey. Start the project describing every detail of your journey at the start and end of your visit. Include any walking you had to do, car journeys to stations, train or plane journeys, or journeys by boat. Say how long each bit of the journey lasted, how far you travelled, how fast you went, what towns you went through and any other sights you saw. You may be able to include tickets, or maps, or pictures of the boat or plane, or other interesting things you got on the journey. (You may want to do work on transport in the place you visit, too: all about the roads, buses, railways, and other ways people travel around the place.)

The place you visit. Where do people live, what are the villages, towns, or cities like, how many people live there, what sort of houses and other buildings are there, are there lots of visitors, are the settlements growing or shrinking, and so on. You may be able to collect postcards or other photos of the places.

Work. What sort of jobs are done? Do people work mostly in primary industries (like farming or fishing), secondary industries (making things in factories), or tertiary industries (like banks and shops, providing a service)? Are there a lot of people unemployed, or working for no money? You may be able to interview someone with an interesting job, and get them to explain what they do, and how they got into that sort of work. What do people do when they are not working — what do they do in their leisure time?

Environment. What is the environment like, and how is it changing? Are there problems in the environment, like pollution or unused buildings or dangerous areas? Is the environment being improved, maybe by building new facilities, or cleaning up old ones? What do people want to improve about the place? (You could interview people, again!)

The landscape. What are the physical features of the area? Mountains, rivers, valleys, seas or oceans, forests and farmland? Try to describe what makes the place different from other places – and try to get as many maps and pictures as possible, to show other people. It would be a good idea to make your own drawings, too.

The climate. You could keep a record of the weather each day, and gradually build up a view of the climate of the place you are visiting. What is the temperature and rainfall? How many hours of sun are there each day? How does the climate affect what people do?

Compare the place you visit with your home region. Go through all the other categories, and try to work out whether they are very different or really quite similar. You could put maps or pictures of the two places side by side. You could describe what things about your home region, or about the place you visited, most surprised you. Or what you liked or hated most in each of the places. Try to explain what is *special* about each place.

History holiday project

The history of the place you visit. Everywhere in the world has a history, just like every person has a life story. It is your job to try to find out what that History is. Here are some of the best sources of information about places.

People who live there. You can ask people who live there what is happening now, and how that is different to what was happening 10, 20, or maybe even 50 or 60 years ago. It is useful to ask old people, but people your own age, who have lived in that place, may know a lot about what the place is like and how it has changed. Remember that people will sometimes disagree about what has happened, or about whether it was good or bad. Try to find out if people have really strong views on issues.

Books. People and libraries may have books about the history of the place. These can make your stay more interesting, as well as helping your History work. See if you can copy out interesting bits from books — stories about famous events or people, or timelines of what has happened over the years. You may be able to get some pictures of famous places or events: the tourist office (if there is one) may be able to help. Try to find out as many things as possible that pupils at your school will find exciting or interesting or useful or horrible.

Buildings and other objects. The history of a place is often in the buildings, statues and parks and place names. Look carefully around the place you visit, and see what clues there are. You may see memorials of wars, or streets named after famous people, or buildings that used to be used by armies, or lots of other things. Ask around, and try to find out the

134

history of the place by studying these objects.

How different is the place you visit to your home region and the UK? Go through all the other categories, and try to work out whether they are very different or really quite similar. You could put pictures or timelines or stories about the two places side by side. You could describe what things about your home region, or about the place you visited, most surprised you. Or what you liked or hated most in each of the places. Are there any historical connections between the two places? Try to explain what is *special* about each place. You might like to invent a time machine, and say what date in the past you would like to visit!

Religion holiday project

People all around the world have beliefs, and many of these beliefs can be based on religion. Try to find out about what important beliefs people have in the place you are visiting. Is religion very important? Are there several religions that people follow? Are there lots of people who don't believe in any religion? Does religion affect people a lot – are there lots of signs of religion, like churches, synagogues, mosques, temples, or shrines? Is the everyday life of the people you are staying with affected by religion? Did you go to any weddings, funerals, or other religious services? Can you describe them, so that when you come back to school you can tell other people about them? Do a survey, and talk to as many people as you can about their beliefs.

Presents

Again, don't worry about getting an 'educational' present if there's something else you or your child would really like, and certainly don't get unwanted presents. However, where you have a choice between two presents, one may be more helpful than another for your child, given the topics and subjects they are studying. Gallery and museum gift shops are often exciting places these days — and I'd like give a special thanks to the Science Museum, where the excellent shop is complemented by a mail order service. Useful presents may include books, and reference books now, for example, are so much more exciting and attractive than they used to be. Equipment, such as musical instruments, art materials, calculators, or computers, can all make good presents, and range in price from the cheap to the massively expensive. A good pen may be loved as much as an expensive computer, although the computer may provide more fun for the whole family. Parents may want to give 'conditional' presents — given if the child passes an exam or does some extra piece of work. There are children who respond well to such bribes, though there is something to be said for giving educational presents to children who are not doing so well, rather than just to the successful.

For all of these possible gifts, I would recommend that the school gives guidance — at least on the topics and subjects that will be studied. Personally, I'd like schools to give out 'possible present' lists, and to set up stalls or bookshops in school, for parents and children to browse around. If this isn't done at your child's school, you could always offer to help set one up, perhaps as a PTA contribution to a Parents Evening. The aim of such activities should be to help parents make decisions and save them time: there should never be a moral pressure on parents to spend money on children, either to save the school money or to substitute for inadequate school equipment. If you never buy your children educational presents in their entire lives, they should be perfectly able to be hugely successful in all their studies.

Television and video

There are plenty of teachers and parents who think that television and videos are educational no-go areas, or even that they are curses to be avoided whenever possible. Amongst the criticisms are that watching television, unlike reading a book, is a passive activity that requires no thought. I'm not so sure. With the number of channels available in many homes, children often 'flick' actively from programme to programme in the same way that people skim through books and newspapers, going back and forth between topics and issues. One person's 'short concentration span' is another person's 'flexibility'. I will admit, too, that over the years I've received as much education from the television as from books — and I'm a real fan of books. There are good and bad television programmes, of course, and most are pretty bad, but the same can be said of books, magazines, and even lessons in school.

Two ways of making good use of television and videos are helping your children decide *what* they watch, and helping them change *how* they watch. On any evening, there will be programmes on topics that will benefit your child. The news, of course, helps with many subjects, especially English and History, but there will also be programmes relevant to Science, Art, Technology, RE, and everything else. It isn't the best advertisement for a programme to say 'this will help you with your school work', so programme makers may hide the obvious relevance of their products, and parents can do more by showing enthusiasm themselves than by forcing an unwilling child to watch something that is 'good for them'. What about the 'how'? Watching television doesn't seem the most skilful activity, but it can be more educational if it is done critically. I'm not saying children should be encouraged to throw things at the screen, but they can be helped to question what they see, to think about the purposes of the programme makers, and to take it all with a pinch of salt. A good game, for example, is to compare soap operas with real life, noting that in soap operas, people almost never go to the toilet or watch the television, and all Australians have long-lost brothers, sisters, parents and children (a forgetful lot, the Australians). Pupils in school dramas don't swear, and in situation comedies, the sofa is always in the middle of the room facing away from the door.

Children are in general very sophisticated viewers, seeing through tricks and false situations, and this sophistication, when encouraged, can help even the worst show be at least a little educational. If you can get (free) tickets for your child to be amongst the audience of a television show, then this is the best possible form of media studies education. Whatever you do, don't assume that television is just filling your child with bad ideas!

Hobbies and work

Most children have hobbies, beyond the television, and schools often know nothing about them. Hobbies have to be voluntary, of course, but parents can help make them available to their children, and can help them be of benefit to schools. If there is a responsible adult involved in the hobby, then you could ask them to write a 'report' on how your child is doing, and pass this report (if good) on to your child's tutor. As a tutor, I find it very difficult wringing information about hobbies out of my tutor group; they are strangely modest about their out of school activities. Hobbies can not only inspire children, they can develop skills and knowledge essential to success in many subjects. A child who seems to do little homework, but has many hobbies, could be learning just as much. As a parent, you can understand this and let the school know, and, if necessary, negotiate ways of balancing homework and hobbies, so that your child's education benefits as much as possible. Perhaps playing an instrument could count as Music homework, or visiting museums could count as (or compensate for poorly completed) History homework.

In later years, in the build-up to GCSEs and beyond, hobbies can become even more important, as the basis of applications for courses and jobs. The hobbies may themselves provide ideas on possible careers, and having a variety of interests is certainly liked by admissions officers and personnel departments. Your child will need to be able to explain why these activities are useful and interesting, and as a parent you can 'rehearse' them in such explanations. The more specific the description the better, so 'being a defender in a Sunday league football team' is better than 'playing football', and 'reading American science fiction novels' is better than 'reading'.

When adults hear people talk about hobbies or 'leisure time', they often say that all their time is taken up with work, whether it is paid work or housework. Some children are in a similar position, perhaps working on Saturdays and on some weekday evenings, or doing housework or caring for other members of their families. As with hobbies, information about such work rarely gets to teachers, and yet it is of enormous value to children's education. Paid work often brings out the 'adult' in children: they may be admirably responsible and mature. Housework and caring may be done skilfully and sensitively. Such achievements are valuable in themselves, and children should be 'credited' with them when it comes to assessing them. Tutors would in general welcome reports from supervisors – perhaps from you as a parent – and could add these to records of achievement. Subject teachers may also like to know. Looking after younger brothers and sisters may be relevant to PE, Technology, English, or much more, depending on what is done. Shop work may benefit Maths or Information Technology, too.

Part 5

Resourcing Homework and Study Support

CHAPTER 27

School libraries and public libraries

It used to be that a library was no more than a place to store books, but now 'library' is too passive a word, really, for the places called libraries, as they are places that have to be used and worked with. 'Flexible learning centre' or 'learning resource centre' certainly sound more active, more like an adventure playground, and, as more people work out what they mean, the names might become more popular. Meanwhile, libraries carry on their work, often under-valued and under-resourced, and, too often, under-used by pupils. Libraries are generally better places to learn than classrooms. The difference between a classroom and a library is like the difference between a ready-made meal and one you cook yourself. The ready-made meal is nourishing enough and can taste very pleasant, but a meal you cook yourself, though sometimes disastrous, can be far better all round, nourishing and memorable. It takes more skill to cook a meal, or use a library well, than it does to heat up a packet, or sit through a lesson.

Libraries can and should be ideal places to support homework, but certain conditions must be fulfilled.

- Timing and access are vital. There are political and economic factors at work here, but the bottom line is that a closed library, or one open at times that pupils can't make good use of, is a waste of resources. School libraries should be able to be staffed before school starts, and after it finishes, long enough for pupils to be able to complete their homework. As homes have such varied resources, having easy access to libraries is an important aspect of equal opportunities in school. Anyway, what could be sadder than a closed library with a pupil outside, unable to do their work?

- Staff in libraries are expected to do increasingly complex jobs. As well as the 'technical' aspects of running a library, the staff are also expected to 'teach', both subjects and the use of the library, and may now be expected to be experts on computers and the Internet. Attitudes are as important as skills, and librarians have had to develop considerable patience with teachers, when 150 children come to the library having been set the homework task 'find out about the Battle of Hastings'. Library staff in schools should train and work closely with teaching staff, and in recent years those working in public libraries have also got more directly involved in school work. Some 'homework centres' (the subject of the next chapter) are situated in school or public libraries, with staff providing 'dedicated time' to helping with projects or computer searches, and this seems an ideal, efficient, way of developing skills and resources.

- Teachers should try to make sure that libraries can provide for the tasks they set as homework, and this could best be done if departments plan homework in advance and let libraries know what will be set. Why not invite the librarian to the department meeting in which homework is planned? If the library can't provide help with homework, how can families?

- Librarians are always trying to improve the resources they have, and teachers can and usually do help choose appropriate ones. A good strategy, used by some libraries, is to get groups of children to choose a certain number of books or other resources to be added to the library. In this way, they may feel more like the library is 'theirs', even if the resources are the same as would have been chosen by teachers or librarians working on their own.

- Although libraries may have thousands of books and other expensive learning resources, the most valuable resource of all may be the tables and chairs. If pupils can work independently, in a space dedicated to learning, then they are half-way to success. Libraries could store 'independent learning' and subject-specialist guides, specific to the school or the local area, and these should be produced by teachers, pupils and library staff working together. Cooperative working could be encouraged, and pupils could practice effective revision techniques. In such ways, pupils will see libraries as places to learn, and not just places to find information.

CHAPTER 28

Homework centres

Homework centres are not new. Recently, however, as, intermittently, in the past, there have been some big initiatives setting them up in schools and communities. The Social Services Committee (not the Education Committee) in Strathclyde funded supported study schemes from 1990 in many of their Primary and Secondary schools, as an anti-deprivation scheme — trying to break what they saw as a cycle of deprivation, in which pupils in poorer areas were more likely to fail in school because of lack of good learning resources at home. Meanwhile in England and Northern Ireland, the Prince's Trust has worked with LEAs to set up similar schemes, and funds have also come from BT, Compact schemes, TVEI, TECs, the European Poverty Fund, NACRO, and various LEAs. No two schemes — of the dozens currently operating — are alike. Some spend their money on staff to keep the library open before the start of the school day and at lunchtimes, some on teachers to staff '4-6' clubs for after-school work; some arrange weekend revision courses, some set up study rooms outside the school but close to where many pupils live. There are as many 'schemes' as there are schemes, and many individual schools have run similar projects for years, quite independently of the Strathclyde and Prince's Trust initiatives.

What all homework centres have in common is a belief that homework should be treated as a central educational issue, and that once you start one of these schemes, the whole school has an opportunity to address its teaching and homework strategies, and its relationship to pupils' homes and families. In some ways, homework centres simply have the advantage of small classes — pupils often say how much they like having the attention of the teachers in these centres. However, small 'classes' in this way can be staffed by non-specialists — including parents who might not have the confidence to help with homework at home. They are therefore more flexible and can involve more members of the community than a simple reduction in class sizes, or hiring private tutors. Other reasons for having homework centres are the effects they can have on the rest of schooling. A survey by John MacBeath suggested that teachers thought benefits would be pupils' study habits, self confidence, and attitudes to independent learning; the actual benefits were in teacher-student relationships, achievement in subjects, and (as expected) study habits. Adults gained a better 'pupil perspective': teachers and pupils understood each other better, parents and pupils understood each other better; the school ethos benefitted, and more equal opportunities were able to be provided.

I've explained the purposes of a homework centre to pupils in this way:

- Why have a homework centre? We all want to do well, pupils, teachers, families, and others in the community. Education needs a lot of hard work. In a classroom, pupils and teachers can work with each other to develop new knowledge and skills. But education also goes on outside the classroom — at home, in local libraries, and elsewhere. We want all the pupils at this school to have the best possible chance to succeed. We want everyone to get the most out of school — to become successful, independent, enthusiastic, learners. The homework centre should make this easier for all of us.

- What happens at the centre? Independent study (which is often called 'homework'!) means finding out for yourself, working hard to learn new knowledge and skills. This can be a difficult business, and it may be tempting to give up at the first problem. If you come to the homework centre, you will find a room with a good working atmosphere. There won't, we hope, be the distractions that stop you working the rest of the time. There will, we hope, be some useful resources — books, tables, chairs, a computer, at least one teacher (who may be able to help you with the work, and will certainly be able to provide a link with the school), and other adults and pupils who want, like you, to make independent learning easier and more successful.

Setting up homework centres can be difficult, and although all the schools who have set them up seem to think they are the best things since sliced bread, all also say they have learnt from their mistakes when setting them up. A good start is a survey of wants — with teachers, pupils, parents and everyone concerned with homework, being surveyed. If funds are available, they could be used mostly on teachers, or on accommodation, or on resources. Whoever is going to be in charge of the centre should think of (and ask about) such issues, and also about transport (can pupils get home safely? will some pupils be unable to get to the centre?), food and entertainment or social activities (useful, but make sure they are separate from the studying), the resources that should be available (most recommend building up resources slowly, according to the wishes of centre users), what staff can be involved (e.g. teachers, library staff, older pupils, student teachers, volunteers from the community, social workers and counsellors) and whether they will be paid. Once set up, how should the centre be advertised — for example, should particular pupils be targeted, perhaps in reports or on Parents Evenings? Such issues are covered, in admirable detail, in the Study Support Resources Pack, produced by Strathclyde and the Prince's Trust (listed in Chapter 34). The theme stressed by that pack, and all the people involved in homework centres, is the need to adapt a centre to the particular needs of the school and its pupils.

A homework centre should complement the help offered in classes and at home, then, so it can't be a good idea 'on its own'. Implications for schools of setting them up include how (and whether) homework is set, what guidance pupils are given, and what resources they may need. Getting all departments involved at an early stage can overcome many difficulties. The 'cardinal principles' reported by one school were: don't think of the homework centre as extra lessons, but as helping with study skills and so on; make sure there is a link to whole school homework policy; use innovative teaching techniques (e.g. visits by authors) so the centre is seen as fashionable not 'swotty'; have competitive interviews for workers, so the managers can get the workers' views out; have very senior teachers in charge, so the scheme has clout; provide food, perhaps, but if you do, then set this up as an enterprise scheme. 'Cardinal sins', from the same people, were: don't force people to attend — staff or pupils; don't restrict non-academic activities, as long as academic activities can also be done; the centre must be well marketed or it will collapse; be prepared to drop staff if they don't fit the ethos of the scheme. Finally, I would recommend that pupils who use such centres should get credit for being so organised.

CHAPTER 29

Community facilities: Beyond homeworking

Homework is at its best when it is more than just extended classwork, and much of this book has looked at ways of helping pupils engage with their homes and families. This should be expanded as much as possible, so that pupils also engage with, and are helped by, other facilities available in their local community and beyond. These facilities vary so much from place to place, and are accessible to different groups of people, that this chapter simply points out some approaches to developing learning in a community, beyond the classroom.

- Community groups, pressure groups, and so on, include specialist educational groups, who aim to improve education in general, and also those who wish to tackle social problems or inequalities, in particular, and try to do this through education. Both kinds of group make a contribution to the learning that goes on in a community, and their contribution is likely to enhance the relevance of that education. We shouldn't forget that controversy surrounds the issue of how much people know, and how they learn: education, as we now think of it, was vigorously fought over. It is often the smaller pressure groups and unions, rather than governments or political parties, that have created the energy for change. Such groups are still fighting: recent changes influenced by this work include the ways schools deal with issues of racism or sexism, or the form of exams for young children, or how schools deal with child abuse. The groups may work outside schools, and may even set up their own schools (usually run on evenings and weekends), and this can increase their independence and distinct influence. They may, however, work with or within schools, and gain the benefits of access to the 'mainstream' and integration with well established institutions. Whether working outside or inside schools, community groups can invigorate, socialise, and politicise; they can raise self-esteem and reduce inequalities. As a teacher I'd like such groups to work with schools, but they must choose where to concentrate their energies.

- Colleges, adult education institutes, and other post-compulsory institutions, are important sources of benefit to children's education, as adult learners not only increase their skills and knowledge, which can be passed on, but also have a greater understanding of the process of learning, which helps everyone. The general progress of children, and the support they get with homework, must be sensitive to the provision of adult education. So helping children may simply mean helping adults.

- Distance learning, both formal, like the Open University, and informal, like educational television programmes, provides learning opportunities for those who would have difficulty accessing full-time education — most obviously those with other jobs or responsibilities. It also provides everyone else with models of independent learning, as I've described in Chapter 2, with the bulk of the learning happening outside 'lessons'.

- Museums, galleries, zoos, farms, factories and fun fairs, these days, nearly all have 'education officers', and all, with or without education officers, are intensely educational. Pupils, teachers, parents and carers should make good use of them all, which means enjoying them, not treating them as worthy shrines to culture or industry. A good rule of thumb: never take a child to a museum or gallery unless you want to go yourself, then, even if the child is bored, at least you'll have enjoyed yourself, and the child will have seen you enjoying yourself.

Communities can in these and many more ways be educative, and can bring out the most positive aspects of homework: engagement with surroundings, and links between the generations.

Part 6
Sharing Information about Homework

CHAPTER 30

Researching homework in schools

Research on homework is surprising, and surprisingly useful. I'm not recommending a huge research project, to be published as a book. Rather, a small piece of research that could be carried out within lesson times by a teacher, student teacher, or even pupils. The best such work I've seen was done by an A Level Sociology student, as part of her coursework. Studies of homework come up with different results, depending on who is questioned. Groups have their own reasons to believe what they believe, but a good bit of research can help everyone.

- Teachers say they set, and pupils do, a lot of homework. Research can help teachers be realistic. Teachers often 'over-set' homework as some pupils will do less than the teacher would like, so that the conscientious pupil will have far too much. Once a teacher knows exactly how much homework pupils do (and should do), they can match tasks to times more accurately. Research can also help teachers to set more interesting and 'possible' homework tasks.
- Pupils say they get, and do, little homework, yet they find the whole business stressful. Research can help reduce pupil stress, and perhaps even increase the amount of homework done. Nearly all pupils find homework a source of stress, especially in Year 10 and above, because they 'feel' the homework even when they are not doing it. A typical afternoon and evening will involve coming back from school at around 4.30 (thinking you need a rest before doing homework), having something to eat (to build up energy for homework), watching the television (and hardly ever thinking about homework), thinking about the evening meal (and not homework), eating (while family members ask you whether you've done your homework), watching the television (with homework becoming more of a worry), worrying about homework (whilst watching television), getting ready to do homework (getting the books out, but not reading them), then, at 10.00 or 11.00, doing an hour's homework. As you finish the homework at 11.00 or

midnight, you will go in to school the next day tired, and complain to your teacher 'I was up till midnight doing this homework'. Research can tell the pupil that, in fact, they only did an hour's homework, and could have finished it all by 5.30 and had the rest of the evening free. It is surprising how different this feels — how much less stressful it is. If they had worked through to 6.00, they would still be less stressed *and* they would have increased their working hours.

- Parents often say the school sets, and their children do, no homework at all. Research can give parents and carers the sort of information they need to be able to deal with the school and their children. Perhaps pupils do indeed get most homework done in school, so they bring home little; perhaps the school thinks it sets a lot of homework but actually, week in, week out, sets very little. Perhaps there's an obvious connection between homework and GCSE results; perhaps (terrifyingly) they are quite unconnected. The more parents and carers know about how teachers and pupils work, the more likely they are to be able to help.

The best research is simple, but simplicity only succeeds when the aims are clear. There are three different types of question that can be asked.

- One question is about the amount of homework set or done. Finding out about quantities is useful as part of a stress-control strategy, and it is useful as a way of avoiding the illusions that teachers and pupils suffer from. The question 'how many minutes/hours do you spend on average doing homework each week?' might get interesting answers, but pupils are often bad at estimating time. Better would be 'in the last seven days, how many minutes/hours did you spend doing homework each day?' Even better, give each pupil a chart with seven days on it (perhaps with each day divided into morning, afternoon and evening), and get them to fill in how many minutes/hours homework are done, day by day, for the next week. It is worth asking about mornings and afternoons even of school days, as much homework gets done at breaktime or during lunch, and older pupils may also have 'private study' time during the day. Will pupils be honest? I've found pupils are more likely to be honest if I ask to look at the homework and say 'well, if you really spent two hours doing that, you must have real difficulties with the subject, though of course if it really took 10 minutes, then it shows you to be really talented, if lazy'. In these circumstances, pupils generally prefer to be thought talented and lazy than slow. (It goes without saying that you wouldn't say any such thing if you thought the pupil had indeed spent hours on the work.)

A recent survey in a London school asked 'trios' of pupils (one achieving at a high level, one achieving at an average level, one achieving less well) how much homework they did. Subject teachers asked them about their own subjects, for five weeks. The results interested me, in that there was no regular pattern to confirm my expectations. Higher achieving pupils didn't systematically do most homework; high-profile subjects didn't automatically get most time spent on them; a significant number of pupils did no homework in several subjects for several weeks, despite the fact that homework had been set and done by other pupils. I'd recommend such a survey as a regular feature of school life: it taught me more about that school than any other figures I might have asked for.

- A second type of question is about homework tasks. This is particularly important if the aim of the research is to make homework more interesting and effective. The simplest form of question asks pupils to describe their favourite homework task, in each subject, and say why the task was so enjoyable. Ask, too, about their least favourite homework tasks set for each subject. Much of Chapters 6 to 11 of this book was based on answers given to these questions. The first conclusion I came to, after asking these questions of a couple of classes, surprised me. Pupils didn't, in general, enjoy easy homework tasks, they preferred hard tasks. They particularly liked the sort of challenging task where they had to think for themselves, and do in-depth research. Most disliked tasks that were routine learning tasks, especially when it was felt that the teacher only set the task because he or she felt obliged to set it.

- A third type of question is about support for homework. It is useful to know whether the biggest barriers to completing homework are the presence of younger brothers and sisters in the home, or the lack of books, or noise, or having too many other household chores. It is equally useful to know whether the school could best help pupils by setting up an after-school homework centre, or by telling parents more about the work done in school, or by allowing pupils to borrow text books or reference books. To get answers to these questions, you could ask about what helps or hinders homework, or what the school could do to help with homework. On after-school clubs, you could ask pupils and parents about how often and for how long they would use, or would like their children to use, such clubs, if they were set up. Should you ask about after-school clubs, it is important to point out that they do not imply more work for pupils: if pupils find it easier to complete homework in these circumstances, it might even reduce the time spent on homework. Having spent over four years working in a homework centre, the thing I most learnt was that pupils actually like getting homework done, and done well. Other teachers and parents could visit such clubs, to find out how they work. (That, too, would be research, especially if the visitors had surveys for the participants to fill in.)

CHAPTER 31

A short guide for teachers (for use in INSET courses)

INSET Guide

INSET on homework could take the form of two sessions. The first activity (described here for teachers from different subjects, though it could be adjusted to suit staff from a single department) is as follows.

> To be done in groups, set up after the task has been described, with the groups formed by numbering everyone in the room (e.g. from 1 to 5) and getting all the number 1s to sit together, and so on.

> All teachers have their own examples of homeworks that have worked well or badly — for all sorts of reasons (some never known) — and this session will try to exploit that knowledge. What is it that makes a homework successful? (Brainstorm from the floor.)

> Each group will look at one key topic from their subjects, and will come up with at least as many successful homeworks as there are people in that group. The aim is to think of different types of homework: at least one oral/aural homework, at least one 'learning' homework, one story or reading homework, one with a cross-curricular significance, one problem-solving exercise (e.g. on the meaning of words), and so on.

> A couple of examples of homework tasks from the groups will be briefly outlined at the end of this first session. For homework, the members of every group will collect or write up full descriptions. The description of a homework will include any essential information about how the homework was set up (e.g. how much of the topic had been done, whether the work was to be started in class), what time and resources would be required by the pupil (in or out of school), and how the homework would be followed up in the next lesson. For example, a homework which was 'learn for a test' would include in the report the test itself (or sample questions), and a description of how pupils could learn for the test — for example how much was learning from their exercise books, how much from textbooks. The homework reports are to be handed in tomorrow, to be duplicated for the whole group. The aim is to have descriptions of half a dozen effective and varied homeworks for every subject or topic.

A second session, on the next day or next week, would go like this.

First, as a homework was set, it would be useful to describe how the homework went. If there is an impression that it went well, then why? If it didn't, then why not? Perhaps individuals who did/didn't do the work could be encouraged to say why — what encouraged or stopped them. Whatever, examples will be written up and discussed. The examples of good homework tasks should be reproduced, so that they can be used by teachers, especially new teachers.

Homework requires the effective cooperation of four groups: teachers/schools, pupils, families/carers and 'resources' (in and out of school). It is worth looking at each of these in turn. Participants could get into groups and decide what advice could be given on each of these issues.

- What do teachers need? They may, for example, need encouragement, guidance, examples or systems. What works best, and how can it be encouraged? A sample of a guide for teachers could be produced for a department or a school. A good guide would include something on how to assess/mark homework, without adding to the burden. A whole-school policy could raise the profile of independent study. Several issues are mentioned in the bibliography, below.
- What do pupils need? How can they be helped to do homework effectively and if possible enthusiastically? Why is or isn't it seen as important? A selection of research (particularly from John MacBeath) is included to help highlight some issues. Does this research change any teachers' views (as it did mine)? What would a guide to pupils include, and could it be supplemented, e.g., by ideal holiday/birthday/ journey work?
- What do parents/carers need? Again a selection of research/quotations is included below. What would a parents' guide look like, and what use would it be?
- What about resources — school libraries, local libraries, books, papers, and so on, including making good use of the resources actually available to real pupils? Work needs to be done on effective distance learning, including the experience of the Open University, and piano lessons.

Policy guide

The following is a guide written for staff, especially useful where staff are unable to do the sort of INSET, above, that might generate the same or similar policies.

Homework is learning that is relevant to the school's curricular objectives, which takes place outside formal classroom teaching, and which is primarily the responsibility of the learner. (Adapted from MacBeath and Turner, 1990.)

'In the past there was, perhaps, a tendency to think of homework in a somewhat restricted way, as being mainly a matter of reinforcement and revision. Its value in this respect will continue to be recognised, but in a school where the general policy is to promote in its pupils characteristics such as personal pride in achievement, initiative and self-confidence, a wider view is likely to prevail.' (NICED, 1989.)

'While 50% of pupils say that they enjoy school, only 2% say that they enjoy homework' (TES, 11/1987).

'The success of homework was related to the quality rather than the quantity of the set assignments' (DES, 1987).

'A poor homework policy and/or practice makes its contribution to enlarging the achievement gap between advantaged and disadvantaged pupils' (Hargreaves, 1984).

'A study found that 94% of homework was given at the end of the lesson, half of the time after the bell had rung, and in 9% of cases during the ringing of the bell' (MacBeath and Turner, 1990).

Homework is an issue of rights and of equal opportunities. Over five years, appropriate homework can add the equivalent of at least one additional year of full-time education — or lacking homework is equivalent to losing one whole year's education. Staff need to work on ways of enhancing homework without setting unreasonable demands on themselves, pupils or families. And not all pupils have the physical facilities and seclusion at home which they need in order to do homework, and some may have other home responsibilities. There are therefore resource implications — books, equipment, school and local libraries. We should appreciate these problems, but at the same time acknowledge the considerable support that can be given by families and others in the home and other resources available outside school (including television). Finally, we should have the same principles guiding homework as we use to guide classwork, of providing stimulating, varied, tasks, adapted to the needs and skills of the pupils.

Some of the chief objectives of homework (according to HMI) are: to encourage pupils to develop the practice of independent study; to develop perseverance and self-discipline; to allow practice, where it is needed, of skills learned in the classroom; to permit more ground to be covered and more rapid progress to be made; to enable class work to concentrate on those activities requiring the teacher's presence; to open up areas of study and to make possible the use of materials and sources of information that are not accessible in the classroom; to involve parents and other adults in pupils' work. 'Where homework involves more than routine tasks, it has at least one of the following characteristics: it is closely integrated with and reinforces classwork and has clear curricular objectives; it exploits the materials and resources in the environment and the community outside the school; it encourages independence, research, creativity and initiative; it promotes the cooperation and involvement of parents and other adults.' Cooperation of parents and carers can, for example, mean setting a task to do at home (like making a snack), with an accompanying questionnaire for parents/carers to fill in.

- All staff agree to set and monitor regular homework, according to the guide in the Staff Handbook and homework timetable. Pupils with long-term absence, or who are excluded, should still be expected to complete appropriate homework tasks. As pupils are expected to complete homework regularly, teachers can reasonably be expected to mark homework regularly.
- Homework should be achievable by all pupils, whatever their levels of skill or home circumstances. If necessary, therefore, homework should be adapted to suit the IEPs and other needs of individual pupils. Credit slips and certificates are available for well-completed homework, and for an improved attitude to homework. If a pupil doesn't complete a homework, it is appropriate to expect them to complete it in school outside lesson times, e.g. in a lunchtime detention.
- Homework should always be relevant to the programme of study and curriculum aims of the subject for which it is set.
- Over a period of time, homework tasks should be varied, to include, for example, investigative work, aural work, preparing for class tests, visits and reading. 'Finishing off' will occasionally be appropriate.
- Homework should positively encourage the support and involvement of parents, carers, and others with whom pupils have contact outside school. This is both a matter of setting tasks that require such involvement (e.g. interviewing relatives about past times), and a matter of giving opportunities for parents and carers to monitor and comment on their children's homework.

CHAPTER 32

A short guide for pupils (for use in Personal and Social Education and study-support time)

We all want to do well — pupils, teachers, families, and others in the community. Education needs a lot of hard work. In a classroom, pupils and teachers can work with each other to develop new knowledge and skills. But education also goes on outside the classroom — at home, in local libraries, and elsewhere. We want all pupils to have the best possible chance to succeed. We want everyone to get the most out of school — to become successful, independent, enthusiastic, learners. Homework can make this easier for all of us.

Independent study (which is often called 'homework'!) means finding out for yourself, working hard to learn new knowledge and skills. This can be a difficult business, and it may be tempting to give up at the first obstacle. You will need a good place to work, with as few distractions as possible, and you will need equipment like pens, pencils and rulers. You will also need to ask parents, carers, and other adults — even older sisters and brothers — to help you at times.

Why do you get homework? The main reason, of course, is to help you learn more. Other reasons are:

- It helps you to learn to work on your own, and use resources outside school. This means you are thinking things out for yourself, and putting them in your own words.
- It teaches you how to plan and organise your work. This helps develop perseverance and self-discipline.
- It gives you the chance to practise what you have done in class, or to do some background work that will help you understand what's coming next. This also helps you make use of outside interests.
- It gives the teacher a chance to check that you have understood the lesson and to find out about any difficulties you are having.
- It involves the people you live with in your work. Parents, carers, and others can help with your work, and can work with the school to help your progress.

Here are some ideas to help you complete your homework successfully.

- Before you do your homework:

    If you think your homework is going to be too difficult, tell your teacher.

    Make sure you know *why* you're doing a particular piece of work.

    If you have a number of different things to do, ask yourself which it is important to do first, second and so on.

- While doing your homework:

    Make sure you have all the books and equipment you need when you sit down to work.

    If possible, work somewhere where nothing can disturb or distract you.

    If something, or someone, distracts you, try to keep concentrating on your work. (Don't get into arguments with annoying brothers or sisters!)

    Don't work for long stretches without a break. Remember that different people work faster or slower, so if your work is taking a very long time, give yourself a short break, and go back to the work with a fresh brain.

    Give yourself a reward when you work. You should be proud of the good work you do!

    Make sure you have some time to do the things you want to do other than studying.

- After doing your homework:

    Read your homework to check that it is something you can be proud of.

    Hand it in on time. Remember that doing work on time is just as important a skill as doing work correctly.

    Now, write down ideas which will help *you* with your homework.

CHAPTER 33

A short guide for parents (for use in preparation for meetings at school)

Introduction

Homework is learning that will help with school work. It takes place outside the classroom, often but not always at home. This is our school's homework policy. As a staff, we have given careful consideration to making homework suitable and well balanced across the school. We believe that properly designed homework can play a valuable part in your child's education. Certainly, over a school career, homework can add a substantial amount of study time. For our policy to be implemented successfully, your support is crucial. If you have any questions about the policy in general, or about your child's homework, please contact the school.

Principles

The same principles guide homework as guide classwork. Homework should be stimulating, including varied tasks, adapted to the needs and skills of the pupils. All pupils should be able to complete homework, whatever their levels of skill or circumstances at home, although all are likely to need encouragement and support to do homework well.

We set homework because:

- it encourages independent study, and the use of resources available outside school;
- it helps develop perseverance and self-discipline;
- it allows practice of skills learned in the classroom, and makes use of outside interests;
- it permits more rapid progress to be made in school;
- it involves parents, carers, and other adults in pupils' work, improving home-school links.

Astonishingly similar report to those done half a century later — including the interesting comparisons of primary and secondary, the disparity between amount of homework perceived by teachers and by pupils, and variation in practice between schools. Based on surveys done from 1935. An example of home conditions: "Except in a few cases the children return home to work in the common living room. Often a meal is in more or less continuous session, the wireless booms and the family chatters. Against such odds, work which might be completed comfortably in a short school period may linger fitfully throughout the evening". Again, half a century before the Strathclyde 'pilots', reference is made to 'homework classes'. These meet after school in the evening, and are under the paid supervision of an assistant teacher.

'Perhaps the most important gain to be won from homework is the development of self-reliance and initiative, where the pupil is left to face unaided a problem suited to his abilities.' 'In this matter of the regulation of homework the importance of securing the cooperation of parents can hardly be exaggerated.'

Great Britain, Department of Education and Science (1985) *Homework. Note by the Department of Education and Science*; London: DES.

A discussion paper following on from the 'Better Schools' White Paper of 1985.

Chief objectives of homework: to encourage pupils to develop the practice of independent study; to develop perseverance and self-discipline; to allow practice, where it is needed, of skills learned in the classroom; to permit more ground to be covered and more rapid progress to be made; to enable class work to concentrate on those activities requiring the teacher's presence; to open up areas of study and to make possible the use of materials and sources of information that are not accessible in the classroom; to involve parents (and other adults) in pupils' work. But, 'The contribution which homework — as an extension of the school day — makes to the pupil's total education needs to be balanced against the other educational opportunities available or utilised at home.' Also, students may find homework frustrating, difficult, meaningless, and unrewarding. Also, 'Not all pupils have the physical facilities and seclusion at home which they need in order to do homework', and some may have other home responsibilities.

Great Britain, Department of Education and Science (1987*) Homework: A Report by HM Inspectors*; London: DES.

160

A follow-up to the previous discussion document, including a survey/results from 243 schools. 'Those schools where homework had greater consistency, purpose and support were generally characterised by the belief that, among the teachers, an effective policy needed to involve not only the senior management team but departmental, pastoral and tutorial staff and be the product of extensive discussion. Moreover the communication of this policy to parents and pupils and, in some cases, the dialogue which this evoked were no less important to the policy's effectiveness than its acceptance by the whole teaching staff.'

Hahn, J. (1985) *'Have You Done Your Homework?': A Parent's Guide to Helping Teenagers Succeed in School*; New York: John Wiley & Sons.

American guide. Some useful bits — like definition of essay terms some of which I've used in Chapter 13. Also work on time management, on research ('term papers'), and on appropriate attitudes of parents to their children's (home)work.

Holmes, M. and Croll, P. (1989) Time spent on homework and academic achievement; *Educational Research,* February, **31** (1).

More time on homework leads to better performance – especially with working class pupils. Reference in MacBeath and Turner (1990).

ILEA (1984*) Improving Secondary Schools: Report of the Committee on the Curriculum and Organisation of Secondary Schools*; London: ILEA.

Known as the Hargreaves Report. Solid, very practical, report. All kinds of ways suggested on analysing and improving education, including overcoming disadvantages deriving from social class, and so on. Homework is covered by section 3.8 on skills for independent learning.

IMPACT (1992) *Ruling the Margins: Problematising Parental Involvement: Submitted conference papers, 23rd-24th September 1992*; London: University of North London, London University Institute of Education.

Collection of academic papers on parents-and-schools, covering key issues of implications of any involvement, contracts, styles of work. Hard to read at times, and all rather theoretical — but all important and sharp, too.

IMPACT Project (1994) *Maths Photocopiables: Impact Maths Homework: Holiday Activities*; Leamington Spa: Scholastic.

One of a big series of books from the IMPACT project, for Key Stages 1 and 2. Scholastic, too, have a long list of photocopy-friendly books for more-or-less harassed teachers. This one is good for parents/carers wanting to help their children learn 'real' mathematics, without sending parent or child asleep. For example, a 'cricket' game for long journeys based on car registration numbers, with runs scored for even numbers, fours scored by numbers divisible by four. The exercises could be used at any time, not just in holidays. I'd have loved them when I was young, and they are quite fun now.

La Métais, J. (1985) *Homework Policy and Practice in Selected European Countries;* Brussels: Eurydice Central Unit.

Comparative study. Reference in MacBeath and Turner (1990).

MacBeath, J. (1993) *A Place for Success: An Evaluation of Study Support in England Scotland and Northern Ireland*; London: The Prince's Trust.

Place-by-place analysis of study support (homework) centres. Great reading with perceptive analysis.

MacBeath, J. and Turner, M. (1990) *Learning Out of School: Report of Research Study carried out at Jordanhill Colle*ge; Glasgow: Jordanhill College.

Probably the central text on homework and how it is (or could/should be) approached. Definition: learning 'that is relevant to teachers' curricular objectives ... which takes place outwith formal classroom teaching ... which is primarily the responsibility of the learner himself/herself'. This study was based on 13 varied Scottish (primary and secondary) schools. Note that 'A school's credibility in the community is often considerably affected by its approach to homework'.

McBride, P. (1994) *Study Skills for Success: Practical Tips for Homework, Projects, GCSEs and GNVQs*; Cambridge: Hobsons/CRAC.

Extremely detailed, rather prescriptive, guide for 13–16 year-olds. Full of checklists and tick lists and hints. Some sections are not so much study skills as straightforward subject skills. Good work, for example, on grammar and spelling. I think that, perhaps, any pupil able to read the book would probably be doing okay anyway. That's the trouble with guides for pupils!

Møller, V. (1994) *Township Youth and their Homework*; Pretoria, South Africa: HSRC.

Interesting account of the role of homework in the development of South African communities in recent times. Case studies of pupils, as well as results of more systematic research. Interesting particulary in showing the social significance of homework.

National Council for Educational Technology (1990) *Developing Partnerships between Librarians and Teachers in Flexible Learning;* Coventry: NCET.

A well-produced pack, more a training manual than just a 'position paper', which goes well beyond the rather narrow title, and should stimulate good discussion amongst all manner of teachers and their non-teaching colleagues.

National Extension College (1985) *Flexible Learning in Small Fifth and Sixth Forms;* Cambridge: National Extension College Trust Ltd.

The NEC produces what used to be called correspondence course materials — well, they may still be called this. The report, by Pamela Harding, looks at the potential of these materials in schools.

Northern Ireland Council for Educational Development (1989) *A School Homework Policy: Primary Guidelines Support Paper;* Belfast: NICED.

Professional opinion is divided on how useful homework is — with the Department of Education for Northern Ireland saying (1981/15) 'It remains the opinion of the Department that formal homework is not essential for pupils in primary schools and preparatory departments ... Homework will be seen as an opportunity not only to practise skills already taught in school but also as a chance to foster social and aesthetic values such as group cooperation, civic responsibility, appreciation of beauty and the enjoyment of leisure pursuits.' Homework should be enjoyable. Parents should be partners.

Office for Standards in Education (1995) *Homework in Primary and Secondary Schools;* London: HMSO.

Not always exciting, but a useful 35 pages.

Rutter, M., Maughan, B., Mortimore, P. and Ouston, J. (1979) *Fifteen Thousand Hours: Secondary Schools and their Effect on Children;* London: Open Books.

On the topic of homework, as on many other topics, there is plenty of information. These findings 'do not show how and why homework is associated with better outcomes. But it may well be that in addition to its practical value in providing opportunities for the consolidation of the learning of work introduced in school time, homework may also be of symbolic importance in emphasising the school's concern for academic progress, and its expectation that pupils have the ability and self-discipline needed to work without direct supervision.'

Salmon, P. (1992) *Achieving a PhD — Ten Students' Experience;* Stoke-on-Trent: Trentham.

A realistic book — a book of problems and not just of successes. A PhD is the biggest homework challenge of all: a couple of dozen 'supervision' sessions, perhaps, or the equivalent of a week of full-time schooling, leading to an 80 000-word thesis. At the heart of this book is an approach to supervision of research students, involving group work with a diverse set of researchers who support each other in ways similar to those of group therapy. A good model for group work of many kinds.

Scholastic Publications Ltd (Editor Noel Pritchard, materials collated and rewritten by Ruth Merttens and Ros Leather, of the IMPACT Project at the University of North London) (1993) *Number: Impact Maths Homework: Key Stage One Photocopiables*; Leamington Spa: Scholastic.

A nice book of maths homeworks, with instructions to parents/carers, and references to National Curriculum attainment targets, etc. Looks like fun, for young children.

Skynner, R. and Cleese, J. (1983) *Families and How to Survive Them*; London: Methuen.

A fine book, helpful and jolly, concentrating on the real meanings of behaviour in relationships. For adults, but interesting for children to read, too. Leave it lying around the house. Homework, in the sense of work done in homes, if you let the book affect you. A good basis for much PSE work, although pupils may well go 'eughh' at a lot of the explanations.

Stern, L. J. (1995) *Learning to Teach: A Guide for School-Based Initial and In-Service Training*; London: David Fulton Publishers.

A guide to teaching, schools and educational research for those involved in training – both students and tutors and researcher-practitioners. Lots of detail on various aspects of teaching and researching education.

Topping, K. J. (1986) *Parents as Educators: Training Parents to Teach Their Children*; London: Croom Helm.

The book, by an Educational Psychologist, deals, in particular, with 'problem' issues — SEN, ethnicity and so on. Chapter 3 is on home-school reporting.

TVEI (1989) *TVEI Developments 10: Flexible Learning;* Sheffield: Training Agency.

A set of brief articles, mostly describing good practice in flexible learning — including the use of (information) technology, libraries and

164

resource-based learning. Good to get an overview of student-centred learning in practice. 'By giving the student increasing responsibility for his or her own learning within a framework of support, teachers will find that, as well as learning the discrete school subjects, students will also develop a range of personal, social, information handling and learning-to-learn skills which considerably enhance personal effectiveness and help contribute to equalise and optimise opportunities for them' (Trayers).

University of Strathclyde Quality in Education Centre for Research and Consultancy, in association with the Strathclyde Regional Council Department of Education (1993) *Study Support Resources Pack*; London: The Prince's Trust.

Videos and study booklet – how to promote, set up and run a study support centre. An expensive pack, worth every penny. (It incorporates MacBeath, 1993.)

Waterhouse, P. (1988) *Supported Self-Study: An Introduction for Teachers*; London: Council for Educational Technology.

A good general guide.

Weller, B. (Ed) (1996) *One Hundred (Mathematics) Homeworks*; Northampton: Paxton Press.

Useful ideas pitched at Year 7 pupils, but useful for other years, too. Many imaginative ideas partly, at least, because it was produced from suggestions of student teachers.

Welsh Consumer Council (1985) *WCC's response to 'Homework' — A Consultation Paper from the Department of Education and Science*; Cardiff: WCC.

A report that stresses the need for partnership between parents and the providers of the educational service. Homework, it says, is the third most cited area of concern of parents about their children's education.

Wooton, M. (1992) *Homework: Pratical Guidance for New Teachers in Secondary Schools* (On Your Own in the Classroom, Booklet No. 12); Upminster: Nightingale Teaching Consultancy.

Good, realistic and, as it claims, pratical guide to setting and monitoring homework, including, unusually, a recognition of the various roles homework may have for parents as well as for teachers. (Hence, for example, 'don't you have any homework' may be a way of getting a child to turn the music down.) Only 10 pages of guidance, but impressively straightforward booklet.

Index